11·12·79

C. S. Lewis
on
Scripture

C. S. Lewis, who may well be the greatest Christian writer of the 20th Century, knew the Bible as literary scholar, devout believer, and well-read follower of the Christian theological tradition. Praised by literary critics for his wit, imagination, and intellect, Lewis is admired most of all for the clarity and conviction with which he treats the basic themes of Christian faith.

In this readable and stimulating new study, Michael J. Christensen provides the first close look at C. S. Lewis's views on Scripture. He devotes the opening chapter to the ever-present debate over the inspiration of the Bible, then goes on to examine Lewis's thinking on myth, revelation, and Scripture, and on understanding the Bible as inspired literature.

Christensen calls attention to the richness of Lewis's approach to Scripture, revealing him as a writer who cannot be labeled either fundamentalist or liberal, who transcends the conventional pigeonholes and dead-end thought traps while expanding theological categories and elevating the realm of discourse about Scripture.

By illuminating Lewis's opinions, Christensen sheds significant light on the current controversies about authority, inspiration, and inerrancy, presenting

Lewis's views as a moderating position that can bring together divergent views. Christensen also shapes some worthy questions of his own: Is C. S. Lewis a romantic or a rationalist? What are the limits of language in conveying truth? How important is imagination in understanding the Bible?

One mark of an original thinker is to put together old ideas in new ways. In a time when originality is often confused with being either iconoclastic or merely different, C. S. Lewis stands as one of the true originals of our age. Michael Christensen has produced an insightful study of this outstanding Christian that will be of interest to layman and scholar alike.

C. S. Lewis
on
Scripture

His Thoughts on the Nature of Biblical
Inspiration, the Role of Revelation
and the Question of Inerrancy

Michael J. Christensen

Preface by Owen Barfield
Introduction by Clyde S. Kilby

WORD BOOKS
PUBLISHER
WACO, TEXAS

C. S. Lewis on Scripture

Printed in the United States of America

ISBN #0-8499-0115-4
Library of Congress catalog card number: 78-65810

All Scripture quotations, unless otherwise noted, are from the Revised
Standard Version of the Bible, copyrighted 1946, 1952, © 1971, 1973
by the Division of Christian Education of the National Council of the
Churches of Christ in the U.S.A., and are used by permission.

Grateful acknowledgment is also made to the following:

Dr. Corbin S. Carnell, University of Florida, for the text of a letter
from C. S. Lewis, and permission to print it.

The C. S. Lewis Estate for permission to include the letters from C. S.
Lewis to Dr. Clyde S. Kilby (May 7, 1959) and to Dr. Corbin S.
Carnell (April 4, 1953). The letters are copyrighted by the Trustees of
the Estate of C. S. Lewis.

The C. S. Lewis Estate and Wm. B. Eerdmans Publishing Co., for
permission to quote the poem "Footnote to All Prayers" from The Pilgrim's Regress, copyrighted by the Trustees of the Estate of C. S. Lewis.

Harcourt Brace Jovanovich, Inc. for permission to quote from "The
Birth of Language" and "Reason" in Poems by C. S. Lewis, edited by
Walter Hooper, published by Harcourt Brace Jovanovich, Inc., copy-
right © 1964 by the Executors of the Estate of C. S. Lewis.

Macmillan Publishing Co., Inc., for permission to quote excerpts from
Mere Christianity by C. S. Lewis, copyright 1943, 1945, 1952 by the
Macmillan Publishing Co., Inc.

TO MOM AND DAD

who taught me to take seriously the
Word of God

Contents

Foreword

Many books have been written and are still being written about the work and thought of C. S. Lewis. But none of them, as far as I am aware, has focused explicitly on its relation to Holy Writ. Lewis always insisted that he was no systematic theologian. Yet he had thought deeply on questions with which theologians concern themselves, such as the distinction between a belief in the inspiration of the Bible and a belief in its verbal inspiration, and as a consequence he had many illuminating things to say about them. Some of these have found their sporadic way into anthologies. In Mr. Christensen's book however they appear grouped round a single nucleus, which is in fact its theme; namely, an attempt to answer the question: What did Lewis believe about the Bible?

That, to my mind, is its outstanding merit. All the more so because on to that question he brings to bear an intimate acquaintance not only with Lewis the Christian apologist, but also with Lewis the literary critic and Lewis the student and lover of myth. This is not only a book to be pondered by fundamentalists and evangelicals engaged in a "battle of the Bible," but one which must appeal to all admirers of that truly astonishing mind. I welcome it especially for the way in which it brings out the stedfast intellectual unity underlying Lewis's utterances on every topic to which he addressed himself, including some as apparently diverse from one another as the Incarnation and the right way to read novels.

OWEN BARFIELD

Introduction

C. S. Lewis is increasingly read by literally millions of people around the world. He is read because he has profound things to say and says them with strength and grace. Paradoxically, Lewis is an original not after the modern fashion of seeking originality and a name but by a profound desire simply to recapture, in all their original meaning, the old platitudes. Many theologians and philosophers are finding in him evidences of true greatness of mind and spirit. He is a thinker with a warm heart.

It is obvious that Mr. Christensen has caught some of these qualities in his own study, especially the element of clear and explicit statement. Also I find here the best perspective I have yet seen for a true interpretation of Lewis's beliefs about God and the Bible, a perspective much needed. Few of Lewis's most enthusiastic followers have noted the importance of placing those beliefs within the immediate context of Lewis as university don and literary scholar and thus understanding such profound subjects as metaphor and mythology as elements in his theology. It is altogether too easy for good Christians to forget that the Bible comes to us not as systematic theology but as great literature.

It is also apparent that the author of this work is well acquainted not only with the books of C. S. Lewis but also with theological backgrounds going back to the church fathers. Thus it is a work that I can recommend with pleasure.

CLYDE S. KILBY

Preface

I am not a scholar but a student. I write not about abstract theological notions but about a subject that concerns scholar and student alike: In what way is the Bible inspired? Are there errors in Scripture? How is God's truth revealed?

I do not pretend to write authoritatively on these questions. I am too young, as well as deficient in academic credentials, and entirely unknown as an author. However, I do happen to know a lot about C. S. Lewis, a man of profound insight whose view of Scripture deserves consideration.

My purpose in writing *C. S. Lewis on Scripture* is to explore the mind of one great scholar in light of the present theological controversy over biblical inerrancy.

This book was begun as a research project during my senior year at Point Loma College. The professors who directed and evaluated the project—Drs. Glenn Sadler, Frank Carver, and Fordyce Bennett—encouraged me to seek publication of my study. I owe them a special debt of gratitude, particularly Dr. Sadler, whose love for literature and Lewis greatly influenced me.

The problem in writing a book about Lewis's view of Scripture is that he never proposed a systematic theory. Though he alluded in his writings to biblical inspiration, he never directly addressed himself to the question of inerrancy. Only in a personal letter to Dr. Clyde Kilby did he admit to having "tentative thoughts" on the subject. Consequently, any conclusions concerning his approach to Scripture had to be drawn from his basic religious assumptions and the way he handled Scripture in his published works.

In my research I attempted to get behind Lewis's articulated religious beliefs to his fundamental assumptions regarding the nature of the Bible. After analyzing relevant parts of his theology, his theory of literature, his understanding of myth and revelation, I applied his basic assumptions to Scripture. Then, by interpreting his "tentative thoughts" I believe I was able to draw inductively some valid conclusions regarding his view of biblical inspiration. In the process, implications regarding the present controversy over inerrancy became apparent.

If this book can shed any light on the issue of inerrancy or help move the evangelical constituency closer to a mediating position on Scripture, then it will have realized its goal and purpose.

I want to thank especially Dr. Clyde Kilby for his personal encouragement to me in the research and writing of this book. His willingness to write the Introduction in the midst of his full schedule is deeply appreciated. I should also like to thank Mr. Owen Barfield for his willingness to read the manuscript and to write the Foreword. I am also grateful to my typists— Paula Jones, Denise Householder and Paul Conant—for persevering through the many revisions. I am particularly indebted to my friend Jim Rutz for his beneficial editorial comments in reviewing the manuscript. And finally, my father, Dr. Val J. Christensen, deserves special thanks for serving as my spiritual counselor, academic mentor, editorial advisor, friend and loved one.

Much work and prayer have gone into these pages. May the Spirit of God lead the reader into all truth.

MICHAEL J. CHRISTENSEN

-1-

In What Way
Is the Bible Inspired?

If every good and perfect gift comes from the Father of
Lights then all true and edifying writings, whether in
Scripture or not, must be *in some sense* inspired.
                              —Letter from Lewis, May 7, 1959 [1]

Pilgrim's Progress is a true and edifying writing. In what sense
is it inspired? The Holy Bible is a good and perfect gift. In what
way is it inspired? Are there degrees of inspiration, and if so, to
what extent? These are questions that concern every serious-
minded Christian.

The purpose of this book is to explore what C. S. Lewis—
perhaps the greatest defender of Christian faith in the twentieth
century—believed about the Bible as compared to other great
literature. In the process we shall draw some conclusions about
the nature of revelation and the question of biblical inerrancy.

The decade of the 70s has seen a surge of debate about the
question of biblical inerrancy. Harold Lindsell and Francis
Schaeffer have been largely responsible for popularizing a controversy which has been raging in theological circles for some
time. The so-called battle for the Bible is particularly violent on
the evangelical front. Some evangelicals insist that "the Bible
is without error in all that it affirms" (including science, history,
biographical facts, and figures).[2] Other dedicated evangelicals
assert that inerrancy has meaning only when applied to the

inherent *teaching* of Scripture in matters of "faith and practice." [3]

Evangelical writers such as Lindsell and Schaeffer have attempted to make scriptural inerrancy a watershed issue. "He who denies the doctrine of infallibility," Lindsell declares, "cannot truly be an evangelical." [4] In a similar spirit Schaeffer has often stated that evangelicals must "draw the line with love and tears" at the point of belief in inerrancy, even if it results in a cleavage in the ranks. [5]

Paralleling, yet apparently unrelated to this growing controversy over inerrancy has been the increasing popularity of C. S. Lewis in evangelical circles. Author of over fifty books, Oxford scholar, Cambridge professor, literary critic, and Christian apologist, Lewis has made a profound impact on contemporary Christianity. "Most of my books are evangelistic," he acknowledged. [6] Hailed as "an unorthodox defender of orthodoxy," "the apostle to the skeptics," and "the most popular and influential Christian apologist of our time," [7] it is quite fashionable these days to quote Lewis on any number of theological subjects as an authority approaching that of a church father.

Given the current theological debate over inerrancy and Lewis's stature and renown in Christian circles, his thoughts on Scripture are of considerable interest. But before we consider them, let us examine the problem. Why all the fuss over inerrancy?

ARE THERE ERRORS IN THE BIBLE?

Perhaps *error* is too strong a word to be applied to Scripture. Yet the Bible, quite frankly, is not without its problems when it is interpreted within a literal and legalistic frame of mind. Several problematic areas can easily be identified:

There are historical problems. For example, how did Judas kill himself? Matthew 27:3 records that he threw his money at the feet of the priests and went out and hung himself. Acts 1:18 records that Judas bought a field with the money he received and there fell headlong on the ground, his body bursting open and his intestines spilling out.

There are genealogical problems. The genealogy of Jesus in Matthew 1 does not agree with the genealogy of Jesus in Luke 3. Neither does the genealogy of Genesis 4 square with that of Genesis 5.

There are factual problems. According to Matthew there was one angel at Jesus' empty tomb. Mark says it was a young man sitting down. Luke says two men stood by the women and proclaimed the resurrection. And John says two angels sat where the body of Jesus had lain, and appeared only to Mary Magdalene.

There are numerical problems. 2 Samuel 10:18 records that David slew the men of 700 Syrian chariots. 1 Chronicles 19:18, a parallel account, records that David slew the men of 7,000 Syrian chariots.

There are major and minor inconsistencies. Who commanded King David to take a census of Israel—the Lord or Satan? 2 Samuel 24:1 claims "the Lord." 1 Chronicles 21:1 claims "Satan." Whom did the voice from heaven address at the baptism of Jesus? Matthew 3:16 reads, *"This* is my beloved Son, with whom I am well pleased." Luke 3:22 reads, *"Thou* art my beloved Son; with *thee* I am well pleased."

There are theological problems. Consider the theology of Ecclesiastes. Is there really nothing better for a man to do than to eat, drink and be merry (Eccl. 2:24)? Is it true that the fate of the sons of men and the fate of beasts is the same (Eccl. 3:19–21)?

There are moral problems. Is the Psalmist right in asking God to slay his enemies or to bless those who would smash Babylonian babies against the rocks (Ps. 137)? Was Jehu morally justified in shedding the blood of the entire house of Ahab in the territory of Jezreel? In 2 Kings 10:30, the Lord congratulates Jehu on a job well done. In Hosea 1:4, the Lord condemns the house of Jehu for the blood of Jezreel.

Lewis was well aware of the "problems" in Scripture. Some

of the Psalms, he admits, are nothing short of devilish. "It is monstrously simple-minded to read the cursings in the Psalms with no feeling except one of horror at the uncharity of the poets." [8] Even the nihilism of Ecclesiastes has its place in Scripture, says Lewis, for "we get there a clear, cold picture of man's life without God." [9]

The problem areas of Scripture must be faced straightforwardly. In a personal letter to Clyde Kilby on the subject of inerrancy (dated May 7, 1959),[10] Lewis suggests that an adequate theory of divine inspiration ought to account for the following representative difficulties:

"*1*. The distinction which St. Paul makes" between the command he relates as being from the Lord, not from himself, and his advice which he offers from himself, "not the Lord" (1 Cor. 7:10, 12).

"*2*. The apparent inconsistencies between the genealogies in Matt. i and Luke iii. Between the accounts of the death of Judas in Matt. xxvii 5 and Acts i. 18–19.

"*3*. St. Luke's own account of how he obtained his matter (i. 1–4).

"*4*. The universally admitted unhistoricity (I do not say, of course, falsity) of at least some narratives in scripture (the parables), which may well extend also to Jonah and Job.

"*5*. If every good and perfect gift comes from the Father of Lights then all true and edifying writings, whether in scripture or not, must be *in some sense* inspired."

6. The paradoxical phenomenon of divine inspiration operating "in a wicked man without his knowing it," so that he utters "the untruth he intends . . . *as well as* truth he does not intend." (See John 11:49–52.)

To Lewis's logical mind, difficulties (2) and (4) would "rule out the view that every statement in scripture must be *historical* truth." The remaining four difficulties negate the view that all parts of the Bible are equally inspired. If Numbers 1:17–46 contains a numerical error concerning the size of Israel, for example, "which in view of the size of the country, if true, in-

volves continuous miracle," it ought not to be used to negate the
inspired record of the resurrection of Christ. The kind of truth
we demand of Scripture, Lewis remarks in conclusion to this
letter, "was, in my opinion, never even envisaged by the
ancients."

The nature of biblical inspiration has been understood in
varying ways by Christians throughout history. Those who
acknowledge special revelation—the grand presupposition that
God has taken the initiative and revealed his truth to man—
differ in their understanding of what this means. The issue is
not whether the Bible is inspired or not, but rather, in what
way? What do the terms *inspiration, infallibility, inerrancy,
revelation,* and *authority* mean? The starting point of the in-
quiry is the internal witness of Scripture itself.

WHAT DOES THE BIBLE SAY ABOUT ITSELF?

"All scripture is inspired by God," according to 2 Timothy
3:16, indicating the ultimate authorship of Paul's own
writing. The Scriptures declare themselves to be the product of
the creative activity of divine "breath" (from the Greek *the-
opneustos,* meaning "God-breathed"). Since God breathed and
man received, God, not man, is responsible for its being. For
this reason the context of the verse asserts that Scripture is
"profitable for teaching, for reproof, for correction, and for
training in righteousness."

We are also told in 2 Peter 1:20-21 that "no prophecy of
scripture is a matter of one's own interpretation, because no
prophecy ever came by the impulse of man, but men moved by
the Holy Spirit spoke from God." Again, it is affirmed that it is
God the Holy Spirit who is the initiator of prophecy and
revelation.

The term *revelation* (with related words) is used throughout
Scripture. When Simon Peter declared Jesus to be "the Christ,
the Son of the living God," Jesus said that "flesh and blood has
not revealed this to you, but my Father who is in heaven"
(Matt. 16:16, 17). Paul says in Galatians 1:11, 12 that the

gospel he preaches is not from man "but it came through a revelation of Jesus Christ." Divine revelation is always "through the Spirit," as 1 Corinthians 2:10 indicates, "for the Spirit searches everything, even the depths of God."

From these scriptural passages and others, it is apparent that *revelation* refers to the activity of God by which he discloses himself and his purposes to men of faith. *Inspiration* refers to the influence of the Holy Spirit on the minds of men to allow them to comprehend and communicate that which is divinely disclosed.

Though the various biblical writers corroborate each other in their statements on divine inspiration and revelation, the questions of inerrancy and infallibility are not specifically addressed in Scripture. Theologians from ancient to modern times have differed widely on these issues as well as in their understanding of how the Bible came to be inspired and how to interpret that which has been revealed. (Chapter 5 is devoted to a brief examination of historical approaches to biblical inspiration.)

REVELATION: PERSONAL ENCOUNTER OR PROPOSITIONAL TRUTH?

Although evangelicals quarrel over the meaning of scriptural inerrancy, the basic issue that divides so-called liberals from most conservatives is the critical question of the nature of revelation. Does the Bible primarily portray instances of subjective encounters with the Divine or does it primarily present objective information about God in conceptual-verbal form? Is the divine revelation essentially personal or propositional?

If revelation is fundamentally known through personal experience, as neoorthodoxy claims, then Christian faith is a positive response to a mystical encounter with the Divine. If revelation is essentially propositional communication from God, as most conservatives maintain, then faith is an acknowledgment of God's authority in Scripture and trust in his divine person which Scripture reveals.

On the battle front in this controversy over inspiration and inerrancy, the liberals affirm the authority of their experience which validates Scripture, while conservatives affirm the authority and infallibility of Scripture which validates their experience. Conservatives charge the liberals with substituting an "inspired experience" for inspired Scripture. Liberals accuse conservatives of "bibliolatry"—diverting to Scripture honor due only to God. The battle over the Bible may be represented in dialogue form as follows:

LIBERAL: Textual criticism has shown belief in biblical infallibility to be completely untenable.

CONSERVATIVE: To discredit Scripture is to discredit God and how he has chosen to reveal himself.

LIBERAL: Then your faith is in the *Bible*, not in the One whom the Bible is about.

CONSERVATIVE: We honor God precisely by honoring Scripture as his written Word.

LIBERAL: But the Bible cannot be equated with the word of God. God discloses himself, not information about himself. The Bible simply contains, becomes and points to the Living Word.

CONSERVATIVE: If the Bible is not itself God's Word written, if there is no revealed objective truth in Scripture, then how can God's Word be known?

LIBERAL: By personal encounter with the Divine. As the song goes, "You ask me how I know He lives; He lives within my heart."

CONSERVATIVE: Then your faith is based on a subjective experience. How do you know if your private perception is objectively true? How can you be certain that your experience of revelation is really of God?

LIBERAL: That's the risk of faith—betting your life that there really is a God, that he cares, that he reveals himself, and that our response to what we conceive to be God is truly God.

CONSERVATIVE: Then what you're saying is that the only standard you have for testing your own subjective, fallible judgment is your own subjective, fallible judgment!

LIBERAL: What else do we have? There is no objective, infallible, eternally secure reference point of truth save God himself. And God, in order to be known, must be experienced individually. In the same way, the Bible is known to be true and meaningful only when God speaks through it.

CONSERVATIVE: The truth of Scripture does not depend on its meaningfulness to those who read and understand it. It is the written Word of God whether people recognize it as such or not! Mankind does not need a book whose fallible words are only a witness to some nebulous "Word." Man needs a Book whose very words are the Word of God.

WHERE DOES LEWIS STAND?

These are tough issues. Definite answers are not easily found. Having distinguished (admittedly too simplistically) between the so-called liberal and conservative positions, we can now proceed to inquire where Lewis stands and what his perspective is on the subject.

Lewis repeatedly declared that he was not a theologian. When he spoke on theological matters, he always qualified himself as an amateur: "I have no claim to speak as an expert in any of the studies involved," he states modestly in *The World's Last Night and Other Essays*, "and merely put forward the reflections which have arisen in my own mind and have seemed to me (perhaps wrongly) to be helpful. They are all submitted to the correction of wiser heads." [11] His remark in the essay "Transposition" is also representative of his attitude: "I walk *in mirabilibus supra me* and submit all to the verdict of real theologians." [12]

Lewis wrote on theological topics because he felt that most theologians failed to do their jobs. He saw his chief role in Christianity as "that of a *translator*—one turning Christian doctrine . . . into the vernacular." [13] As an apologist this meant writing in a lucid style simple enough for the common man to attend to and understand. "If the real theologians had tackled this laborious work of translation about a hundred years ago, when they began to lose touch with the people (for whom Christ died)," Lewis sensibly states, "there would have been no place for me." [14]

Though he addressed countless theological subjects, Lewis never offered a systematic appraisal of the nature of Scripture. By his own admission in a personal letter (already discussed) he had only "tentative" thoughts on the subject. He alluded sometimes to inspiration in his writings but never directly addressed himself to the question of scriptural inerrancy. The issue simply did not assume for him the monumental importance it currently receives in religious circles.

To get beyond Lewis's articulated religious beliefs to his fundamental assumptions regarding the nature of Scripture, we must give thoughtful analysis to (1) his provocative theological persuasions and speculative sentiments, which suggest his view of Scripture, (2) his theory of the function of literature and the role of literary criticism, which largely determine his approach to biblical literature, and (3) his appreciation of myth (properly defined) and understanding of revelation, which apply directly to the Bible. From these three critical areas of discussion we will make an attempt to interpret Lewis's thoughts on Scripture, inductively draw some conclusions regarding his view of inspiration, and relate his position to the issues identified in this chapter. Some implications for the present controversy over inerrancy should then become apparent.

–2–

Lewis: Liberal or Conservative?

I have been suspected of being what is called a Fundamentalist.

—*Reflections on the Psalms*[1]

Liberals accuse him of being fundamentalist. Fundamentalists
accuse him of being liberal. How are we, then, to understand
Lewis's "mere" Christianity? Does he lean toward the right or
the left on the theological spectrum?

Conservatives are uneasy about the liberal nature of some of
his beliefs, his tendency to speculate on religious matters, and
his candid recognition of the problems in Scripture. Liberal
scholars fault him for his rejection of historical skepticism, his
relentless defense of the supernatural, his a priori rejection of
modern theology, and his supposed ignorance of responsible
biblical criticism. It should come as no surprise, then, to find
Lewis difficult to classify.

A widely read Christian scholar, Lewis does not confine his
religious views to the Bible but recognizes God's revelation in
literary masterpieces, in other religions, in ancient world myths,
and through human reason and intuition. Christianity is true,
he seems to say, not just because the Bible says so but because
God chooses to reveal himself through many different ways, yet
supremely through Christ. This liberated perspective leads

Lewis to a degree of tolerance of other beliefs and lifestyles in Christianity as well as in other religions.

Such religious views of Lewis often arouse concern from fundamentalist Christians. Edgar Boss is one theologian who surveyed Lewis's theological writings and attempted to evaluate him in terms of his adherence to or deviation from orthodox Christian doctrines. Boss questions Lewis's orthodoxy in respect to his belief in purgatory and the nature of Holy Communion. He is also disturbed by Lewis's supposed acceptance of organic evolution, the "example theory" of Christ's atonement, and elements of higher criticism of Scripture.[2]

No attempt will be made in this chapter to systematize Lewis's theology. Rather, those views which make Lewis open to various charges of unorthodoxy by concerned Christians, as well as his orthodox views, will be summarized. Note: the purpose in examining some of Lewis's controversial thoughts is to begin identifying his underlying attitude toward Scripture which exposes itself through his articulated religious beliefs.

RELIGIOUS TOLERANCE: WE ARE NOT TO JUDGE

Some Christians will be inclined to label Lewis liberal on the basis of his tolerant attitude toward things like beer, tobacco and the cinema. In expounding on the meaning of the cardinal virtue of temperance, Lewis says, "An individual Christian may see fit to give up all sorts of things for special reasons—marriage, or meat, or beer, or the cinema; but the moment he starts saying the things are bad in themselves, or looking down his nose at other people who do use them, he has taken the wrong turning.[3]

As a Christian, Lewis also remains somewhat tolerant of other religions; at least he did not conclude that all other religions are totally wrong in what they believe. Some religions are closer to the truth than others, and even the most peculiar religions, he supposes, "contain at least some hint of the truth." [4] The fact is, Lewis insists, that God has not told us what his arrangements are for those in other religions. While maintaining that the only way to the Father is through the Son, he adds, "we do not know that only those who know Him can be saved through Him."[5]

In his fairy tale for children, *The Last Battle,* Lewis seems to speculate on what God's arrangements might be for those in other religions. In the last days of Narnia after the last battle had been fought, we meet Emeth, the young Calormene prince. He hated the name of Aslan, the true ruler of Narnia who was a Lion, and worshiped the false god Tash. In the afterlife, Emeth entered the heavenly stable expecting to meet Tash. Instead, he found himself in the Kingdom of Aslan, and was greeted, not by Tash, but by the great Lion himself. Emeth relates what happened:

> ". . . the Glorious One bent down his golden head and touched my forehead with his tongue and said, Son, thou art welcome. But I said, Alas, Lord, I am no son of thine but the servant of Tash. He answered, Child, all the service thou hast done to Tash, I account as service done to me. . . . no service which is vile can be done to me, and none which is not vile can be done to him. Therefore if any man swear by Tash and keep his oath for the oath's sake, it is by me that he has truly sworn, though he know it not, and it is I who reward him. And if any man do a cruelty in my name, then, though he says the name Aslan, it is Tash whom he serves and by Tash his deed is accepted. . . . But I said . . . I have been seeking Tash all my days. Beloved, said the Glorious One, unless thy desire had been for me thou wouldst not have sought so long and so truly. *For all find what they truly seek.*"[6]

Though salvation comes only through Christ, Lewis reminds us not to conclude that only those who explicitly accept him in this life are truly being saved. Legitimate religious experience transcends superficial appearances. Instead of labeling people as either Christians or non-Christians, Lewis would encourage us to appreciate Christianity in the context of developmental process:

> There are people (a great many of them) who are slowly ceasing to be Christians but who still call themselves by that name: some of them are clergymen. There are other people who are slowly becoming Christians though they do not yet call themselves so.

There are people who do not accept the full Christian doctrine about Christ but who are so strongly attracted by Him that they are His in a much deeper sense than they themselves understand. There are people in other religions who are being led by God's secret influence to concentrate on those parts of their religion which are in agreement with Christianity, and who thus belong to Christ without knowing it. . . . And always, of course, there are a great many people who are just confused in mind and have a lot of inconsistent beliefs all jumbled up together. Consequently, it is not much use trying to make judgments about Christians and non-Christians in the mass.

HEAVEN AND HELL: THE CHOICE IS OURS

Closely related to Lewis's theology of salvation is his concept of heaven and hell. He viewed human beings as being on the road of life progressing toward a state of heaven or hell. Each moral choice we make furthers us along the road and slowly changes us into a more heavenly or a hellish creature. In *Mere Christianity*, Lewis describes this process:

. . . every time you make a choice you are turning the central part of you, the part of you that chooses, into something a little different from what it was before. And taking your life as a whole, with all your innumerable choices, all your life long you are slowly turning this central thing either into a heavenly creature or into a hellish creature: either into a creature that is in harmony with God, and with other creatures, and with itself, or else into one that is in a state of war and hatred with God, and with its fellow-creatures, and with itself. To be the one kind of creature is heaven: that is, it is joy and peace and knowledge and power. To be the other means madness, horror, idiocy, rage, impotence, and eternal loneliness. Each of us at each moment is progressing to the one state or the other.[8]

It is significant that for Lewis, hell is not a place God sends people who disbelieve the gospel, but a state of mind one chooses to possess and become. "And every state of mind, left to itself," he writes, "every shutting up of the creature within the dungeon of its own mind—is, in the end, Hell."[9] Yet hell is

more than a state of mind. It is "the darkness outside" heaven—
"the outer rim where being fades away into nonentity." [10]

Hell is intolerable, not from its own perspective, but from
heaven's point of view. The damned really do not wish to escape
their nocturnal habitat; the cost would be too great. "Milton was
right," says Lewis's Teacher in *The Great Divorce*. "The choice
of every lost soul can be expressed in the words 'Better to reign
in Hell than serve in Heaven.' There is always something they
insist on keeping, even at the price of misery." [11] Yet by God's
grace the gates of heaven are eternally open to any who would
repent and believe the gospel. If the damned choose not to enter
in, it is truly by their own will, for "the doors of hell are locked
on the *inside*." [12] Concerning the wicked man's soul, we are "to
hope that he may, in this world or another, be cured." [13]

In *The Great Divorce* Lewis imaginatively portrays his belief
in what other Christians might regard as a second chance: "You
have been in Hell," a bright Spirit says to a ghost from hell,
"though if you don't go back you may call it Purgatory." [14]
Those who choose to go back (as most do in the allegory) or to
remain within the locked doors of hell (as is more likely the
case) God cannot redeem. God wills that none should perish
but that all should gain eternal life, yet all *will not* be saved. In
creating beings with freedom, God submits to the possibility of
defeat. The damned are successful rebels to the finish. "There
are only two kinds of people in the end," says Lewis—"those
who say to God, 'Thy will be done,' and those to whom God
says, in the end, *'Thy* will be done.' " [15] To those who question
God's goodness in allowing the possibility of hell, Lewis returns
the question:

> In the long run the answer to all those who object to the doctrine
> of hell is itself a question: "What are you asking God to do?" To
> wipe out their past sins and, at all costs, to give them a fresh
> start, smoothing every difficulty and offering every miraculous
> help? But He has done so, on Calvary. To forgive them? They
> will not be forgiven. To leave them alone? Alas, I am afraid that
> is what He does. [16]

PURGATORY: OUR SOULS DEMAND IT

Lewis's conviction that Christianity is a process, that people are potential gods or devils who will one day rule in heaven or hell, necessitated for him a belief in purgatory.[17] Some may regard such belief as "unorthodox," but Lewis was in essential harmony with his Anglican orthodox tradition.

To accept Christ as Lord, Lewis understands, is to submit to the full treatment for sin, which necessarily involves purgation. This is why Christ warned those who would be his disciples to "count the cost." In *Mere Christianity*, Lewis offers a convincing paraphrase of Christ's words:

> "Make no mistake," He says, "if you let me, I will make you perfect. The moment you put yourself in My hands, that is what you are in for. Nothing less, or other, than that. You have free will, and if you choose, you can push Me away. But if you do not push me away, understand that I am going to see this job through. Whatever suffering it may cost you in your earthly life, whatever inconceivable purification it may cost you after death, whatever it costs Me, I will never rest, nor let you rest, until you are literally perfect. . . ." [18]

For Lewis, purgatory is a place of purification of the saints where, at the very gates of heaven, the saved soul "begs to be taken away and cleansed." [19] He elaborates on this theme in *The Great Divorce*, depicting souls from hell visiting the purgatorial outskirts of heaven, counting the cost, and deciding whether they wish to remain or not. The moral choice involved is great: "If we insist on keeping Hell (or even earth) we shall not see Heaven: if we accept Heaven we shall not be able to retain even the smallest and most intimate souvenirs of Hell." [20]

Belief in purgatory led Lewis to offer up prayers for the dead, another theological notion which is no doubt regarded by some as a departure from the road of Protestantism, but again, not out of harmony with his church's teaching and practice. He believed also in praying to the saints. "If you can ask for the prayers of the living," he reasons, "why should you not ask for the prayers of the dead?" [21] Lewis admits that the traditional Protestant view of the afterlife is that one is either damned or saved and that prayer for the dead is equally useless either way. But he retorts, "Our souls *demand* Purgatory, don't they?" [22]

If the end result of the Christian life is complete conformity to Christ's image (Rom. 8:29), and if the One who began the good work in us will see it through to completion (Phil. 1:6), then God's sanctifying efforts must continue after death, at least for most of us. If we are to be literally perfect as our Father in heaven is perfect (Matt. 5:48), then purgatory, Lewis deduces, is a logical necessity.

THE EUCHARIST: THE VERY LIFE AND GRACE OF GOD

Lewis might also be on shaky evangelical Protestant ground regarding the Eucharist. As indicated in the section "What Christians Believe" (*Mere Christianity*), "there are three things that spread the Christ life to us: baptism, belief, and that mysterious action which different Christians call by different names —Holy Communion, the Mass, the Lord's Supper." [23]

Lewis supposes that his ideas about Holy Communion "would probably be called 'magical' by a good many modern theologians." [24] He believes in the "real" presence of Christ when Christians partake worthily of the Lord's Supper. The physical bread and wine are "transposed" into spiritual vehicles that carry the very life and grace of God. "The veil between the worlds," says Lewis, referring to the natural and supernatural realms, "is nowhere else so thin and permeable to divine operation. Here a hand from the hidden country touches not only my soul but my body." [25]

Lewis admits that he doesn't understand the "magical" or mystical nature of Communion. Some people, he says, seem to be able to discuss different theories of the sacrament as if they understood them all and were free to choose which one they thought best. But this he cannot do. The divine command, after all, was "Take, eat," not "Take, understand." [26]

THEISTIC EVOLUTION: ANIMAL RAISED TO HIGHER LIFE

Whatever view Lewis holds of Scripture, however he understands the doctrine of creation, the theory of organic evolution caused him no problems. Modern science claims that man descended from animals and that the first men were "savage brutes." Fine. If *primitive* rather than *barbaric* is meant by the term *brute*, then Lewis has no objection to the scientific view.[27] What he adamantly objects to is the notion of "emergent evolution"—that man is naturally progressing upwards toward perfection and complete knowledge.

Lewis perceives man as animal raised to higher life by the purpose and power of God. In *The Problem of Pain*, he discusses the doctrine of the Fall of man and offers a "not unlikely tale," that is, a "myth" in the Socratic sense, of what might have been the case:

> For long centuries God perfected the animal form which was to become the vehicle of humanity and the image of Himself. He gave it hands whose thumb could be applied to each of the fingers, and jaws and teeth and throat capable of articulation, and a brain sufficiently complex to execute all the material motions whereby rational thought is incarnated. The creature may have existed for ages in this state before it became man. . . .

But it was only animal, though it might have been resourceful enough to make and use tools which archeologists would later interpret as proof of its humanity. "In the fullness of time," however, God generated in this organism "a new kind of consciousness which could say 'I' and 'me,' which knew God, . . . which could make judgements of truth, beauty, and goodness. . . ." And so man became a living soul in the image and likeness of God. His name was Adam and his home called Eden.

Regarding the essential goodness of early man, Lewis states: "I do not doubt that if the Paradisal man could now appear among us, we should regard him as an utter savage, a creature to be exploited or, at best, patronized. Only one or two, and those the holiest among us, would glance a second time at the naked, shaggy-bearded, slow-spoken creature: but they, after a few minutes, would fall at his feet."

No one knows, of course, how many of such creatures God made, nor the duration of their paradisal state. But sooner or later they became corrupted. Tempted to become as gods—"to call their souls their own"—human desire found expression. "This act of self-will on the part of the creature, which constitutes an utter falseness to its true creaturely position, is the only sin that can be conceived as the Fall." [28]

Thus man evolved and fell. In Lewis's theology, evolution is still going on—both toward and away from the Creator. At the source of the process is God, "in Christ reconciling the world to himself" (2 Cor. 5:19).

IMMORTALITY OF ANIMALS:
A HEAVEN FOR MOSQUITOES?

If Lewis too willingly accepts the Darwinian thesis of man's ascent from the beasts, perhaps it is because he holds a high view of animals in general. A strong antivivisectionist, Lewis speculates that animals may have immortal souls. In the chapter "Animal Pain" in *The Problem of Pain*, Lewis suggests this possibility and finds himself in company not only with "old maids" but with the great reformer John Wesley, according to his footnote.

Those who seriously object to Lewis's speculation may point to the complete silence of Scripture and Christian tradition. But Scripture, he states, and it is important to note, doesn't claim to answer all questions posed by man. The curtain of truth has been torn at one edge "to reveal our immediate practical necessities and not to satisfy our intellectual curiosity."

The theory Lewis suggests (and again, it is only a theory) is that animal immortality is related to the immortality of man. In the same way that Scripture speaks of Christ "in" God and man "in" Christ, so animal may be "in" man. Man was ordained by God to have dominion over the animal kingdom in the same way that Christ rules the church. "If a good sheepdog," for example, "seems 'almost human' that is because a good shepherd has made it so." And if certain animals have immortal souls, their immortality lies "not in themselves, but in the immortality of their masters." And to any who scoff at the possibility of an animal resurrection with the question, "Where will you put all the mosquitos?" Lewis replies in kind: "A heaven for mosquitos and a hell for men could very conveniently be combined." [29]

CHRIST'S ATONEMENT: FACT AND THEORIES

Lewis's unique approach to the Atonement may also disturb some Christians who, as he once did, regard one particular understanding of Christ's death as essential Christianity. The traditional view Lewis was asked by Christians to accept was the doctrine of a just God bound by nature to punish sin, but because Christ volunteered to be punished in our stead, God let us off the hook.

Lewis gradually came to realize that theories *about* Christ's death were not as important as the *fact* of his death. Many theories have been advanced by Christians as to what the Atonement means (e.g., penal substitution, limited atonement, vicarious atonement, ransom to the Devil, satisfaction theory, moral influence theory), but theories are not to be confused with the reality itself. As Lewis says, "A man can accept what Christ has done without knowing how it works." Any explanation of the Atonement is at best only a reasonable approximation. Doctrinal statements never quite square with the absolute reality. In this context Lewis offers his opinions on the subject.

The meaning of Christ's death for Lewis is in its exemplary demonstration of divine repentance. Jesus died on the cross to show us how we are to die to our fallen natural selves. Repentance, says Lewis, "is not something God demands of you before He will take you back and which He could let you off if He chose; it is simply a description of what going back is like." We need to repent, explains Lewis, but are helpless to do so without God. We need God's help "to do something which God, in His own nature, never does at all—to surrender, to suffer, to submit, to die." But because God became man, we can go to the cross with him. Christ, as the perfect sacrifice, died for us so that we might undergo spiritual death and be raised to eternal life.[30]

Thoughts such as these have been conceptualized and labeled (rather weakly) the "example theory" of the Atonement, which is the label Edgar Boss employed to describe Lewis's theology. Lewis reminds us, however, that it is at best only a theory. If it does not help we are advised to "drop it." The crucial thing is to accept that which Christ accomplished on the cross:

> Of course, you can express this in all sorts of different ways. You can say that Christ died for our sins. You may say that the Father has forgiven us because Christ has done for us what we ought to have done. You may say that we are washed in the blood of the Lamb. You may say that Christ has defeated death. They are all true. If any of them do not appeal to you, leave it alone and get on with the formula that does. And, whatever you do, do not start quarrelling with other people because they use a different formula from yours.[31]

Is the Bible Historically True?

Lewis is sometimes charged with being an occasional friend of higher criticism. In *Reflections on the Psalms* Lewis frankly admits that he does not believe every sentence in the Old Testament contains historical or scientific truth "any more than St. Jerome did when he said that Moses described Creation 'after the manner of a popular poet' (as we should say, mythically) or than Calvin did when he doubted whether the story of Job were history or fiction." [32]

It makes little difference to Lewis whether the story of Ruth, for example, is historical or not. "I've no reason to suppose it is *not*," he says.[33] Either way, the truth of the story is inspired and acts on us as the Word of God. Nor does he have any theological difficulty in accepting Genesis as "derived from earlier Semitic stories which were Pagan and mythical." [34] But because the creation story has mythic qualities does not mean it is untrue. Myth can be truer than historical fact.

The Adam and Eve tale, for instance, may express poetically the reality of man's fall from perfection better than any strictly historical account possibly could. Was the forbidden fruit symbolic, then? "For all I can see, it might have concerned the literal eating of a fruit," says Lewis, "but the question is of no consequence." [35] Clyde S. Kilby, an acknowledged authority on C. S. Lewis, states that "Lewis's frequent discussions of the Garden of Eden make it apparent that it means a hundred times more to him as myth than it does to most Christians as history." [36]

The value of some biblical accounts (e.g., of the Resurrection), depends very much on whether the events actually happened, Lewis maintains, "but the value of others (e.g., the fate of Lot's wife) hardly at all. And the ones whose historicity matters are, as God's will, those where it is plain." [37]

Regarding the question of the general historical accuracy of the New Testament, Lewis concludes that the evidence is in its favor. He cites Jesus' expectation of his return within the lifetime of his disciples ("This generation shall not pass, till all these things be done," Mark 13:30, kjv), side by side with Christ's confession of ignorance ("But of that day and that hour knoweth no man, no, not the angels which are in heaven, neither the Son, but the Father," Mark 13:32, kjv). The early Christians believed that the Second Coming would occur in their lifetime. Jesus seemed to have told them so. But Christ did not return when they expected and, in truth, he knew no more about when the world would end than anyone else. Lewis perceives the apparent contradiction of Christ's words as substantial evidence that the records are historically trustworthy:

> Unless the reporter were perfectly honest he would never have recorded the confession of ignorance at all; he could have had no motive for doing so except a desire to tell the whole truth. And unless later the copyists were equally honest they would never have preserved the (apparently) mistaken prediction about "this

generation" after the passage of time had shown the (apparent) mistake.

The evidence is convincing, Lewis concludes from these and other scriptural passages, that the New Testament is historically reliable: "The evangelists have the first great characteristic of honest witnesses: they mention facts which are, at first sight, damaging to their main contention." [38]

BIBLICAL CRITICISM: FRIEND OR FOE?

While it is true that Lewis accepts some of the conclusions of higher criticism, he generally distrusts the critics.

In his essay, "Modern Theology and Biblical Criticism," Lewis charges most critics with a lack of literary judgment. He cites as an example, a commentary in which the author regards the Fourth Gospel as a "spiritual romance"—"a poem, not a history." Lewis responds: "If he tells me that something in a Gospel is legend or romance, I want to know how many legends and romances he has read, how well his palate is trained in detecting them by the flavour; not how many years he has spent on that Gospel."

On such literary grounds, Lewis speaks with greater authority than the biblical critic in question: "I have been reading poems, romances, vision-literature, legends, myths all my life. I know what they are like." Speaking as a qualified literary critic, and not as a theologian or even as a Christian here, Lewis asserts that there are only two possible views about the Fourth Gospel: "Either this is reportage—though it may no doubt contain errors —pretty close up to the facts; nearly as close as Boswell. Or else, some unknown writer in the second century, without known predecessors or successors, suddenly anticipated the whole technique of modern, novelistic, realistic, narrative." [39]

While Lewis heartily endorsed the use of textual criticism in establishing the trustworthiness of biblical documents, he remained skeptical of source criticism. As a literary critic who applied the same principles of interpretation in his field to the critical problems of biblical interpretation, he distrusted the historical/biographical mode of hermeneutics. The attempt to "reconstruct the genesis" of either modern or ancient texts, that is, "what vanished documents each author used, when and where he wrote, with what purposes, under what influences—the whole *Sitz im Leben* of the text," was to Lewis irrelevant and dangerously misleading.[40]

Source criticism may appear quite innocent and convincing, Lewis admits. He might have been convinced himself if it were not for the painful experience of watching determined reviewers ruthlessly reconstructing the supposed genesis of his own books. "Until you come to be reviewed yourself, you would never believe how little of an ordinary review is taken up by criticism in the strict sense: by evaluation, praise, or censure, of the book actually written. Most of it is taken up with imaginary histories of the process by which you wrote it."

For instance, early in his career, Lewis published *Rehabilitations and Other Essays* in which he included an essay on William Morris, an essay "I really cared about and in which I discharged a keen enthusiasm." One reviewer proclaimed confidently that the essay was the only one in the collection in which Lewis felt no interest. Says Lewis, "The critic was, I now believe, quite right in thinking it the worst essay in the book; at least everyone agreed with him. Where he was totally wrong was in his imaginary history of the causes which produced its dullness."

After that time Lewis noted with interest and concern similar source studies of his own books as well as those of his friends with whose real history he was familiar. His impression was that the record of the critics is one hundred percent in error: "You would expect that by mere chance they would hit as often as they miss. But . . . I can't remember a single hit."

Lewis goes on to cite the example of the Ring in J. R. R. Tolkien's *The Lord of the Rings,* which many reviewers said was suggested by the atom bomb. "What could be more plausible?" asks Lewis. "Here is a book published when everyone was preoccupied by that sinister invention; here in the centre of the book is a weapon which it seems madness to throw away yet fatal to use. Yet in fact, the chronology of the book's composition makes the theory impossible."

Another example is that of a reviewer who attributed the Tiger in one of Roger Lancelyn Green's fairy tales to the influence of Lewis's Lion in his Narnian tales. "In reality, this is not so, and is chronologically impossible," Lewis emphatically states. "The Tiger was an old inhabitant, and his land a familiar haunt, of Mr. Green's imagination long before I began writing."

Lewis argues that the fallacious quality of historical reconstructions of contemporary texts, whose facts *can* be verified, casts considerable doubt on the validity of critical methods applied to ancient ones where no such verification is possible. "The 'assured results of modern scholarship', as to the way in which an old book was written, are 'assured'," Lewis concludes, "only because the men who knew the facts are dead and can't blow the gaff."

What implications can be drawn, then, as to the value of contributions by biblical scholars who dedicate their lives to source criticism of ancient texts? Lewis speaks forthrightly: "While I respect the learning of great biblical critics, I am not yet persuaded that their judgment is equally to be respected." [41]

MODERN THEOLOGY: CHRISTIANITY-AND-WATER

Despite his religious speculations, occasional appearances of unorthodoxy, and departures from theological conservatism, C. S. Lewis in no way identifies himself with what he calls "Liberal Christianity." In his Preface to *Mere Christianity*, as well as in his other writings, Lewis clearly states his adherence to and defense of common or "mere" Christianity. To identify with the traditional certitudes of Christian faith is to be at odds with much of modern theology. Some of Lewis's most biting satire, from his earliest writings to his last, is directed against what he believes to be the "watered-down popular theology of modern England." "What makes some theological works like sawdust to me," Lewis explains, "is the way the authors can go on discussing how far certain positions are adjustable to contemporary thought, or beneficial in relation to social problems, or 'have a future' before them, but never squarely ask what grounds we have for supposing them to be true accounts of objective reality." [42]

Richard B. Cunningham, in his book *C. S. Lewis: Defender of the Faith,* conveniently summarizes Lewis's assailment of liberal Christianity:

> In *The Screwtape Letters* he portrays the skeptical vicar and the shocking vicar. The apostate clergyman in *The Great Divorce,* in the guise of intellectual honesty and free inquiry, abandoned the orthodox faith, and in consequence achieved popularity, sales of his books, and a bishopric. In *That Hideous Strength,* one encounters Busby, the ex-clergyman, and Straik, the mad parson, both of whom represent the "religion of naturalism." Mr. Broad in *The Pilgrim's Regress* represents modernizing Christianity that puts more emphasis on the language of the heart than on the lifeless views and barren formulas of mere orthodoxy. All these characters are vivid fictional portrayals of what Lewis calls "Christianity-and-water"—the diluted synthetic religion of liberal Christianity.[43]

In his adamant opposition to modern theological thought, Lewis was the first to admit that he did not speak authoritatively as a qualified theologian. It was only when theologians, or any other professionals, strayed from their specific fields of competence into the realm of general philosophy that he felt he had something worthwhile to offer.

In his essay on biblical criticism (previously discussed), Lewis chides and criticizes biblical scholars and clergymen for offering dogmatic philosophical assumptions as if they were gospel. Originally addressed to a group of theological students in Cambridge from "a sheep, telling shepherds what only a sheep can tell them," the essay identifies a basic problem with liberal Christianity: The "enlightened" clergy cannot very well preach their liberal theology to uninitiated parishioners without disastrous consequences. According to Lewis,

> A theology which denies the historicity of nearly everything in the Gospels to which Christian life and affections and thought

have been fastened for nearly two millennia—which either denies the miraculous altogether or, more strangely, after swallowing the camel of the Resurrection strains at such gnats as the feeding of the multitudes—if offered to the uneducated man can produce only one or other of two effects. It will make him a Roman Catholic or an atheist. What you offer him he will not recognize as Christianity.[44]

Upon hearing, for example, that biblical miracles are really only parables, or that the Resurrection is true only in the spiritual sense, the average layman, Lewis predicts, would do one of two things: Either he would leave a church where Christianity, as he saw it, was no longer preached and look for one where it was, or, if he agreed with the modern version, would no longer call himself a Christian. "In his crude, coarse way," Lewis effectively jabs, "he would respect you much more if you did the same." In *Letters to Malcolm*, Lewis asks, "Did you ever meet, or hear of, anyone who was converted from scepticism to a 'liberal' or 'de-mythologised' Christianity? I think that when unbelievers come in at all, they come in a good deal further."[45]

With sad sarcasm, Lewis identifies the way most liberal priests (and pastors, too) handle their theological dilemma. They embrace a conception of two truths: "a picture-truth which can be preached to the people, and an esoteric truth for use among the clergy."[46] The esoteric truth has little or no space for the supernatural, but is academically acceptable. The picture-truth is an embarrassment and a hindrance which, if it could only be removed, would allow Christians to get on with their real business of love, social action and celebration.

One of the reasons Lewis is suspected by liberals of being a fundamentalist, he claims, is that he refused to regard "any narrative as unhistorical simply on the ground that it includes the miraculous." Lewis's defense of miracles is purely philosophical. "The real reason why I can accept as historical a story in which a miracle occurs is that I have never found any philosophical grounds for the universal negative proposition that miracles do not happen. I have to decide on quite other grounds (if I decide at all) whether a given narrative is historical or not." [47]

Despite charges to the contrary, Lewis was not theologically naïve nor did he refuse "to acquaint himself with responsible Biblical criticism," as one critic charged.[48] It is true that Lewis was unimpressed with modern theology. He determined important theological matters "in terms altogether different from those employed by most pedagogues in university and religious circles," as a more sympathetic critic observed.[49]

LEWIS: LIBERAL, CONSERVATIVE, OR FASCINATING MIXTURE?

Any Christian writer who achieves popular acclaim inevitably becomes controversial. C. S. Lewis is no exception. Richard Cunningham has perceptively written, "Lewis' approach to biblical criticism offers a middle ground between radical criticism and literalism. Consequently, he can please neither the liberal nor the conservative." [50] Attacked by both liberal theologians and Christian fundamentalists, Lewis's uncompromising defense of "mere" Christianity remains steadfast. A self-confessed romantic converted to Christianity halfway through life, he is neither theologically liberal nor conservative; he defies classification.

Perhaps the reason Lewis defies classification is his unsystematic approach to religious truth. He makes no attempt to construct an elaborate and logical system that accounts for all evidence. Instead he offers the basic facts, and his perception of the facts, or sometimes his tentative thoughts about the facts. Paul Holmer, professor of theology at Yale Divinity School, observes, "Lewis' discovery of Christianity was plainly a rather momentous event for him. But he seems not to have been converted to a theological scheme at all, and he refused all his life to think that an understanding of Christianity would necessitate that he adopt an elaborate theology." [51]

In keeping with his fundamental posture not to embrace a

particular theology or system of beliefs about God or his written word, we must not be surprised to find him offering only tentative thoughts on matters such as the nature of biblical inspiration and inerrancy.

To understand Lewis's thoughts on the divine inspiration of biblical literature, we must first consider his appreciation of literature in general.

–3–

Literary Criticism of the Bible

> . . . an author should never conceive himself as bring-
> ing into existence beauty or wisdom which did not exist
> before, but simply and solely as trying to embody in
> terms of his own art some reflection of eternal Beauty
> and Wisdom.
>
> —"Christianity and Literature" [1]

Lewis approaches Scripture not as a theologian but as a literary
scholar. It is therefore not surprising to find in his theology elements of literary criticism. If the Bible, as Lewis believes, comes
to us not as systematic theology, but as inspired literature, we
must learn what literature is and then apply our understanding
to the Bible.

Lewis's approach to literature in general can be divided into
four essential parts: (1) the characteristics of the good reader,
(2) the nature of the true poet, (3) the role of the imagination,
and (4) the relationship between language and Ultimate Reality.
With a literary foundation securely laid, Lewis's unique understanding of biblical inspiration will become apparent.

GOOD LITERATURE COMPELS GOOD READING

Traditionally, literary taste has been a matter of the critic's
judgment of the merits of what is read. In *An Experiment in
Criticism*, Lewis reverses this order and proposes that the value
of literature be determined by its effect on the "good reader."

Good literature is that which permits, invites, and often compels good reading. Though literature is primarily an art form to be enjoyed, only a certain kind of reader is capable of enjoying it in Lewis's view. The distinguishing quality of the good reader is his ability to (1) receive the work of art as an end in itself; (2) enter fully into the perspective of the poet, submitting himself to a new way of seeing the world; and (3) allow the poetic images to act on his own imagination, revealing their particular purport and soliciting appropriate emotional responses.

(1) Art of whatever kind can either be received or used. The first characteristic of the good reader is his ability to receive a work of art as an end in itself. To receive what great literature offers is to exert one's "senses and imagination and various other powers according to a pattern invented by the artist," that is, to embrace the imagined reality conveyed by the artist in the way it is intended. To merely use literature is to "treat it as assistance for our own activities," that is, as a subjective springboard to, or substantiation of, personal, preconceived philosophies. The good reader absorbs the magic evoked by the richness of style and language. The poor reader perceives only enough of the content to serve his present need, like one who satisfies his lust rather than entering into the full meaning of sexual love.[2]

The activity of using rather than receiving literature is the common perversion of reading into a particular work meaning that is not intrinsically there. After enjoying subjectively what one gets out of a good poem, Lewis good-humoredly suggests,

> why not go back to the text, this time looking up the hard words, puzzling out the allusions, and discovering that some metrical delights in my first experience were due to my fortunate mis-pronunciations, and see whether I can enjoy the poet's poem, not necessarily instead of, but in addition to, my own one? If I am a man of genius and uninhibited by false modesty I may still think my poem the better of the two. But I could not have discovered this without knowing both.[3]

(2) A second characteristic of the good reader is his capacity to enlarge his being by entering into the perspective of the poet. He is thus able to "see with other eyes, to imagine with other

imaginations, to feel with other hearts," as well as with his own.[4] To properly appreciate literature, Lewis maintains, we must lose ourselves in the activity of reading. Negatively, this means, "we must not let loose our own subjectivity" upon literature. "We must begin by laying aside as completely as we can all our own preconceptions, interests, and associations." As a positive effort, "we must look, and go on looking till we have certainly seen exactly what is there." We come before literature not to manipulate it but to have something done to us. To enjoy art we are called to self-abandonment. "Look. Listen. Receive. Get yourself out of the way." [5]

In the proper reading of literature, Lewis adds, there should be no problem of belief. The skeptic should "suspend his disbelief" and practice "Negative Capability," as Keats urged, grasping the essential nature of the art without trying to force it into a particular mold, logical system, or personal notion. The good reader, according to Lewis, enters fully into the attitudes, feelings, and experiences embodied in the poet's art. In so doing, "I become a thousand men and yet remain myself. Like the night sky in the Greek poem, I see with a myriad eyes, but it is still I who see. Here, as in worship, in love, in moral action, and in knowing, I transcend myself; and am never more myself than when I do." [6]

(3) The third mark of the good reader is a vivid imagination which permits intuitive perception of poetic images and evokes powerful emotional responses. While poor readers read books only "when there is nothing better to do, gobble up each story to 'find out what happened,' and seldom go back to it," good readers read and reread great literature and are "profoundly moved." [7] They allow literature to work its magic on them, trying not to extract meaning but rather opening themselves up to some new aspect of Reality presented in the context of the art.

Lewis, focusing on the characteristics of the good reader rather than on what is read, avoids both the subjective and the chronological heresies. The subjective heresy recognizes artistic beauty only in the eye of the beholder; the chronological heresy determines taste on the basis of what is currently fashionable in literary circles. By observing the effect of reading as a criterion for literary judgment, Lewis finds an objective standard of artistic value: "For the accepted valuation of literary works varies with every change of fashion, but the distinction between attentive and inattentive, obedient and wilful, disinterested and egoistic, modes of reading is permanent; if ever valid, valid everywhere and always." [8] Consequently, the good reader is the only qualified judge of the literary value of a particular book or poem. The burden of proof rests on the author or poet to show that his writing "deserves, because it rewards, alert and disciplined reading." [9]

GOOD POETRY IS ARTISTIC IMITATION OF REALITY

For Lewis, the nature of the true poet, like that of the good reader, is defined in terms of his function. In his essay, "The Personal Heresy in Criticism," Lewis attacks the widely held view of poetry as the expression of the poet's personality. In its place he proposes an objective, impersonal theory which defines poetry as the artistic imitation of reality. The true poet reflects eternal realities in his art. His role is not to point to himself but beyond himself: "The poet is not a man who asks me to look at *him*; he is a man who says 'look at that' and points: the more I follow the pointing of his finger the less I can possibly see of him." [10]

As a classical literary scholar, Lewis reminds us that poets from Homer down to Herrick and Emerson, in composing their poems, appealed for supernatural aid. They sought to express, not their own personalities and ideas, but wisdom from above. They viewed the nature of poetry as the inspired embodiment of objective, transcendent reality:

> From Homer invoking the Muse down to Herrick prosaically noting that every day is not good for verses—from the romantic talking of his "genius" to Emerson declaring that there was a great deal of inspiration in a chest of good tea—they all unequivocally declare that the words . . . will not come for the asking, are rare and wooed with hard labour, are by no means

the normal furniture of the poet's mind, are least of all his own possession, his daily temper and habitual self.[11]

The attempt to read poetry as the creative self-expression of the poet is what Lewis calls "the personal heresy." The approach would be valid, he believes, only if truth were relative and each man free to express his particular existential reality. If reality were nothing more than an interplay of blind, irrational forces, as the materialist essentially claims, then poetry is indeed self-expressive, but at the same time as meaningless as the universe itself. "If, on the other hand," Lewis asserts, "something like Theism or Platonism or Absolute Idealism is true—if the universe is not blind or mechanical, then equally the human individual can have no monopoly in producing poetry. For on this view all is designed, all is significant. . . . The Muse may speak through any instrument she chooses."

In his characteristic either/or dialectic, Lewis delineates the dilemma: "Either there is significance in the whole process of things as well as in human activity, or there is no significance in human activity itself." And if human activity has no significance, if objective truth and morals are but a cosmic bluff, if belief in a transcendental realm is nothing more than wishful thinking, if the universe is devoid of meaning, then so is man and the poetry he produces. But if there is meaning at all, Lewis concludes, then man does not *mean* alone. The source of his inspiration is beyond himself. "Embrace either alternative (universal absurdity or objective truth), and you are free of the personal heresy." [12]

The function of poetry then, for Lewis, is to transport the mind beyond mere language into the imagined realm of the nonverbal and the nonliterary (i.e., the transcendental realm). Poetry is "a little incarnation" giving substance to realities formally invisible. It conveys experiences which the reader recognizes (or through "suspension of disbelief" imaginatively accepts) as true. In its highest form, poetry is an artistic reflection of Ultimate Reality.

Is art, then, merely a vehicle of eternal truth? Not "merely," Lewis points out.[13] The difference between truth conveyed abstractly via philosophy and concretely through literature is, as Sir Philip Sidney observes: Philosophy "teacheth obscurely, so as only the learned can understand," while art (or poetry) "is the food for the tenderest stomachs." [14]

Poetic language—alliteration, vowel-music, figures of speech, images, association—is the means employed to portray artistically those realities and experiences which are perhaps indescribable in ordinary prose. The true poet, says Sidney, "is a man who produces such compositions more often and more successfully than the rest of us." [15]

What Lewis offers us is a choice between two contrary approaches to the nature and function of literature: Either an artist creates "beauty and wisdom which did not exist before," or he embodies "in terms of his own art some reflection of eternal Beauty and Wisdom." The true poet, in Lewis's view, is fundamentally neo-Platonic in outlook. In acknowledging a higher plane of reality, he naturally approaches literature differently from the existentialist poet who affirms only what is real and meaningful to him. The latter aims to express himself through his art. The former seeks to embody universal realities. The existentialist literary critic values creativity and originality in art form. The neo-Platonic critic values eternal Reality and concrete experiences *portrayed in a beautiful way*. The existentialist or "modern" approach to literature is concerned with "art for art's sake." The Platonic or "classical" approach is concerned with art for truth's sake.

Lewis's classical understanding of the function of art is nowhere better portrayed by him than in an episode in *The Great Divorce*. A famous artist is one of many tourists on the bus from hell. Arriving at the outskirts of heaven, the first thing he wants to do is paint the majestic scene. Informed that painting is not necessary, the artist is naturally perplexed. The Spirit tries to explain:

"When you painted on earth—at least in your earlier days—it was because you caught glimpses of Heaven in the earthly landscape. The success of your painting was that it enabled others to see the glimpses, too. But here you are having the real thing itself. It is from here that the messages came. There is no good *telling* us about this country, for we see it already."

The artist was no longer interested in the embodiment of eternal Beauty in terms of his own art, but rather in self-expression. The Spirit perceptively remarks: " 'Every poet and musician and artist, but for Grace, is drawn away from love of the thing he tells, to love of the telling.' " [16]

Lewis's approach to literature presupposes, of course, the existence of universals and particulars in the neo-Platonic sense. It would not be entirely accurate, however, to say that Lewis bases his literary theory on Plato's epistemology. "If there is anything Platonic in my position," he states in *The Personal Heresy*, "I trust I shall argue to it and not from it." [17]

If Lewis (and Plato) are correct in affirming the existence of the two realms—related in such a way that universals are mirrored in the particulars of art, literature and science—then how are transcendent realities revealed? How is knowledge of the ideal dimension obtained? For Lewis, a self-confessed Romantic with mystical tendencies, *imagination is the key.*[18]

A "BAPTIZED IMAGINATION"—THE KEY TO ULTIMATE REALITY

Like Plato and Aristotle, Lewis distinguishes between two kinds of knowledge.[19] *Savoir* is descriptive knowledge *about* Reality, subject to the laws of logic and reason. It is the kind of abstract knowledge available through theories, philosophies, and systems—what some theologians call "propositional truth." *Connaitre*, in contrast, is knowledge *of* Reality, apprehended by acquaintance with and participation in what has often been called the "Divine Logos." A person in touch with Ultimate Reality in the intimate, intuitive, imaginative sense of *connaitre* has access to divine revelation, though his rational interpretation of his experience is subject to distortion and his communication to error.

While science and philosophy are concerned with abstract,

descriptive knowledge of the cosmos, religion is concerned with who man is in relation to who God is, with what is Beautiful, Just and Good. Knowledge of these universals requires divine acquaintance, "some 'tasting' of Love Himself." [20] A "baptized imagination," as Lewis termed the romantic, mystical, intuitive sense, is necessary to obtain essential knowledge of the Ultimate.

Paul Holmer, in his recent study, *C. S. Lewis: The Shape of His Faith and Thought,* has brilliantly analyzed Lewis's epistemology and the nature of his romantic-rational faith. Chapter Two, "On Theories and Literature," is particularly beneficial in identifying Lewis's fundamental assumptions regarding reality, revelation, and knowledge.

Holmer begins by observing that the modern mind-set is accustomed to radical uncertainties. It is fashionable for most professionals to acknowledge the logical validity of numerous incompatible philosophies, any of which might in reality be true: "because we have so many theories, philosophies, and theologies, we are sometimes prone to think they are all about equal and that nothing much can be said that will confirm one over another. Logic and facts 'seem' to be on all sides or none, as the case may be; and 'relativism' and 'indifference' look the better part of sophisticated wisdom." [21]

Our dilemma is in knowing too many theories *about* Reality which hinders our intuitive perception *of* Reality. In trying to analyze Reality we make statements, construct models, and adopt systems to account for the facts. The problem with such conceptualizing efforts is that Reality is too large and complicated to be reduced to absolute propositions and systems. All statements, concepts and theories about Reality fall short of what they seek to capture. The more one defines and conceptualizes, the more abstract the truth becomes. One soon loses the very object of his perception. As Lewis observes, "Human intellect is incurably abstract. . . . As thinkers we are cut off from what we think about." [22]

As an Oxford scholar well-versed in philosophy and literature, Lewis, too, often felt the skepticism that inevitably arises from familiarity with a variety of views on a particular subject. But he resisted the attitude of indecisiveness which settles for holding the options open, awaiting confirmation one way or another. Lewis's epistemology, according to Holmer, is not simply that all systems and theories are wrong, but that no statement, no theory, no system is quite adequate in expressing the Ultimate. The organ of Reality, says Holmer, "is not quite the hypothesis nor wholly the metaphysical theorem." [23] If we think truth is there, we beg the question, which hypothesis? or what theorem? There are too many theories and too much evidence in support of each. "There is no correct theory," Holmer adds, "because no theory at all can suffice. Something radically different is needed." [24]

The radically different approach to Reality which is needed is more intuitive than scientific, more experiential than analytic. This is where imaginative literature comes to our aid and offers an alternative to our systematic perplexity. According to Holmer, "Literature is not a disguised theory, nor an implied didacticism. Instead, it communicates in such a way that, when successful, it creates new capabilities and capacities, powers and a kind of roominess in the human personality. One becomes susceptible to new competencies, new functions, new pathos and possibilities." [25]

Unlike philosophy and science which are concerned with the abstract analysis of Reality, imaginative literature functions to bring us into contact with universal realities. It creates thoughts in us, arouses emotions, desires, and hopes we did not know we had, and allows us to *taste* what is real. Through imaginative literature, says Holmer, "another kind of 'seeing' and 'hearing' is open to us all. . . . It is as if there is finally an everlasting truth and an indefeasible grasp of things that is open to anyone who is both logical and romantic, sensitive and cogent." [26]

In so far as literature activates the imaginative faculty to perceive Reality in all its complexity, irony, and paradoxical significance, it achieves its purpose. Through a "baptized imagination," one can bypass all the countless theories, philosophies and points of view *about* Reality and, as Plato said, "look straight at Reality." [27]

HUMAN LANGUAGE FALLS SHORT OF THE
REALITY IT SEEKS TO DESCRIBE

So dim below these symbols show,
Bony and abstract every one.
Yet if true verse but lift the curse,
They feel in dreams their native Sun.
—"The Birth of Language" [28]

Transcendent Reality, when envisioned by the imagination, does not readily adapt itself to interpretation and communication, as Lewis recognizes in his poem, "The Birth of Language." Religious experience, for example, is difficult if not impossible to conceptualize and express in ordinary language. When one tries to communicate meaning which has been experienced and imaginatively received, there arises immediately the problem of language. If we are to convey our experiences at all, we must, as Thomas Aquinas suggested, use ordinary language in an extraordinary way. We must employ poetry, analogy, and the language of religion.

The "language of religion," Lewis says in his essay by the same title, is not the language of science or philosophy, but somewhere in between the language of ordinary conversation and the language of poetry. He is careful to distinguish between these types. To convey the experience of coldness, for example, scientific language might offer, "It was 13 degrees Fahrenheit." Ordinary language might simply offer, "It was very cold." The language of poetry might put it this way: " 'Ah, bitter chill it was! The owl for all his feathers was a-cold; The hare limped trembling through the frozen grass, And silent was the flock in wholly fold: Numb'd were the Beadsman's fingers.' " [29]

From these three representative statements, we begin to understand both the limitation and the imaginative power of language. Scientific language is inadequate in conveying how cold it was. Its function is to deal only with measurable facts and precise descriptions, not to appeal to the imagination. Ordinary language comes closer to conveying the notion of coldness, and the language of poetry closest of all. Of course, all language is problematic in that it falls far short of the actual experience being conveyed. Language can only point, allude, approximate, signify, and help one imagine what it is like. As Lewis says,

> This is the most remarkable of the powers of Poetic language: to convey to us the quality of experiences which we have not had, or perhaps can never have, to use factors within our experience so that they become pointers to something outside our experience—as two or more roads on a map show us where a town that is off the map must lie.[30]

Lewis applies this understanding of the function of language to "God-talk." To convey religious experience of Ultimate Reality, ordinary language would relate, "I believe in God." Abstract theological language, akin to that of science, might communicate, "I believe in incorporeal entity, personal in the sense that it can be the subject and object of love, on which all other entities are unilaterally dependent." Religious language, which comes close at times to poetical, might portray the object of religious experience as "the God of love," "the ground of our being," "the Father of lights," "our heavenly Father," or "the everlasting arms." Such analogous language, though limited, is imaginatively powerful and informative, but informative "only to those who will meet [it] half-way," with "a certain readiness to find meaning." [31]

Lewis's friend, Owen Barfield, in his essay "Poetic Diction," also analyzes the nature and function of language. There is "magic," he says, in the richness of imaginative language (whether religious or poetic) which not only provides pleasure but leads to new knowledge. It serves to *enlarge* our being as we apprehend reality through our own imagination. It functions to conceptualize our experiences by representing the immaterial in picturable terms.[32] As Lewis summarizes, "The very essence of our life as conscious beings, all day and every day, consists of something which cannot be communicated except by hints, similes, metaphors, and the use of those emotions (themselves not very important) which are pointers to it." [33]

THE HUMAN PREDICAMENT

Language can only *point* to that which cannot be adequately communicated. The reality to which language points must be experienced in order to be known. But even in experience itself there is a human predicament, as Lewis recognizes. "Five senses; an incurably abstract intellect; a haphazardly selective memory; a set of preconceptions and assumptions so numerous that I can never examine more than a minority of them—never become even conscious of them all. How much of total reality can such an apparatus let through?" [34]

We are limited both in our rational faculty for knowing and our linguistic ability to communicate meaning. We can neither apprehend Reality absolutely nor express ourselves exactly. Out of epistemological and semantic necessity we turn to metaphor.

A metaphor is defined as "a figure of speech in which a word or phrase literally denoting one kind of object or idea is used in place of another to suggest a likeness or analogy between them." [35] Metaphor, at best, is a window or a bridge to an idea, a way of imagining what is meant. There is always a discrepancy, however, between the idea meant and the metaphor which suggests it.

Our language, according to philologists, is inescapably metaphoric. In order to discuss anything not empirically observed by the senses, we must rely on metaphors. When a teacher, for example, wishes to explain a difficult concept, he will search for an appropriate metaphor to convey, approximate, or point to the truth of the concept. A teacher, acutely aware of the discrepancy between reality and the metaphor which represents it, always qualifies his use of metaphor, insisting that it must not be pressed too far.

An example Lewis employs from his essay "Bluspels and Flalansferes" is that of the imaginary "Flatlanders" who could only comprehend two dimensions and therefore believed their world was infinitely flat. Were they able to perceive three dimensions they might realize that they did not live on an infinite plane but a finite globe. The image of the "Flatlanders" is analogous to three dimensional creatures, like ourselves, who cannot comprehend the finiteness of space because of our inability to intuit more than three dimensions.

The only way we can talk about the reality of the finiteness of space, or the presence of God, or anything metaphysical, is through useful metaphors analogously suggesting what Reality is like. Though the discrepancy between Reality and language symbols remains, we cannot grasp truth on any other terms; we cannot communicate meaning in any other tongue. "Our only choice," Lewis concludes, "is to use the metaphors and thus to think something, though less than we could wish; or else to be driven by unrecognized metaphors and so think nothing at all." [36]

Feeling helplessly bound to metaphors, even in prayer, Lewis offers a "Footnote to All Prayers":

> He whom I bow to only knows to whom I bow
> When I attempt the ineffable Name, murmuring *Thou*,
> And dream of Pheidian fancies and embrace in heart
> Symbols (I know) which cannot be the thing Thou art.
> Thus always, taken at their word, all prayers blaspheme
> Worshipping with frail images a folk-lore dream,
> And all men in their praying, self-deceived, address
> The coinage of their own unquiet thoughts, unless
> Thou in magnetic mercy to Thyself divert
> Our arrows, aimed unskillfully, beyond desert;
> And all men are idolators, crying unheard
> To a deaf idol, if Thou take them at their word.
>
> Take not, oh Lord, our literal sense. Lord, in Thy great,
> Unbroken speech our limping metaphor translate.[37]

While admitting that human language is helplessly metaphoric, Lewis differs with much of linguistic analysis and philosophy of language in his conviction that metaphoric discourse has a real and objective correlative in the universe.

In *The Pilgrims Regress*, John is confronted with a transcendent "Other"—something "more than a metaphor." A certain Man appears and explains to John the nature of this reality:

"Your life has been saved all this day by crying out to something which you call by many names, and you have said to yourself that you use metaphors."

"Was I wrong, sir?"

"Perhaps not. But you must play fair. If its help is not a metaphor, neither are its commands. If it can answer when you call, then it can speak without your asking. If you can go to it, it can come to you." [38]

Though we see "through a glass darkly," we see clearly enough that God is more than a metaphor. Though limited by human language, we understand enough to take seriously the commandments of God as well as his help and guidance.

We must learn to walk the middle road between agnosticism —total silence about the nature of God and his activity—and absolutism—boxing God into precise definitions and finite conceptions.

The human predicament, on the deepest level, is man trying rationally to understand or consume a Reality which can only be imaginatively envisioned or spiritually tasted. We experience transcendent Reality only in precious moments of mystical encounter. Reality quickly vanishes when "we try to grasp it with discursive reason," as Lewis recognizes. [39] When we attempt to translate tasted Reality into descriptive knowledge (i.e., propositional truth), we get abstraction. "This is our dilemma," he concludes, "either to taste and not to know or to know and not to taste." [40] "Of this tragic dilemma," Lewis says, "myth is the partial solution. In the enjoyment of a great myth we come nearest to experiencing as a concrete what can otherwise be understood only as abstraction." [41]

Good readers, true poets, a baptized imagination, a proper understanding of human language—what have these to do with the nature of biblical inspiration? Simply this: If the function of imaginative literature is to embody in its use of language some reflection of transcendent Reality, then this same function can also be applied to biblical literature, its purpose being to convey religious Reality by pointing through language to divine revelation. Inspired myth, for Lewis, is the best pointer.

–4–

Myth, Revelation and Scripture

"Child, if you will, it *is* mythology. It is but truth, not
fact: an image, not the very real. But then it is My
mythology . . . this is the veil under which I have
chosen to appear even from the first until now. For this
end I made your senses and for this end your imagination, that you might see My face and live."
                                        —*The Pilgrim's Regress* [1]

If the function of imaginative literature and religious language
is to portray metaphorically human experience and allude to
ultimate reality, then what is the best form of metaphor? Given
the problem of knowledge and the problem of language, how
can ultimate reality be revealed? And how does the answer to
these questions relate to the nature of biblical inspiration? We
turn now to a discussion of myth, revelation and Scripture.

We See through a Glass Darkly

The great medieval theologian Thomas Aquinas related to
ultimate reality in the intuitive as well as in the rational sense,
and concluded that human beings can know that God *is* and
that he is his own essence, but we cannot know in any precise,
affirmative sense *what* God's essence is. The attributes of the
Infinite cannot be contained in finite language or thought.
Aquinas also asserted, however, that mankind was not destined
to silence about the Source of his religious experience. We can
speak of God in two ways. We can say what God is not (*via*

negativa), thereby narrowing the possibilities of what he is. We can also approximate the nature of God by employing useful analogies (what can be termed *via analogia*).

(1) The negative approach to knowledge about God assumes that what we call "God" is Something infinite, inscrutable, incomprehensible, and indescribable. Consequently, the only true statement we can make about the nature of God is, in the words of the ancient Upanishad, "neti neti"—not this, not that. By making negative statements, saying what God is not, we can gain a closer and closer approximation of what he is.

(2) The positive approach to knowledge about God is through useful analogies, similes and metaphors. We can say, for example, that God is a "heavenly Father" or the "good shepherd," that Christ is "the Lamb of God" who is "seated at the right hand of the throne of God," or that the kingdom of God is "like a grain of mustard seed," or "like a treasure hidden in a field." The point is that we have no other way to talk about God and the reality of his realm except through allegory, metaphor, symbol and other forms of analogy. Even abstract theological language is hopelessly metaphoric.

Lewis concurs with Aquinas and other theologians who recognize the problem of knowledge as related to the nature of God. In *The Four Loves,* for example, Lewis qualifies the precision with which our finite understanding of love can be related to Love himself: "The precision can, of course, be only that of a model or a symbol, certain to fail us in the long run and, even while we use it, requiring correction from other models." [2] In *Miracles,* he argues that what we call *God* cannot even be conceived apart from metaphoric images:

"I don't believe in a personal God," says one, "but I do believe in a great spiritual force." What he has not noticed is that the word "force" has let in all sorts of images about winds and tides and electricity and gravitation. "I don't believe in a personal God," says another, "but I do believe we are all parts of one great Being which moves and works through us all"—not noticing that he has merely exchanged the image of a fatherly and royal-looking man for the image of some widely extended gas or fluid.

A girl I knew was brought up by "higher thinking" parents to regard God as a perfect "substance"; in later life she realised that this had actually led her to think of Him as something like a vast tapioca pudding. (To make matters worse, she disliked tapioca.) We may feel ourselves quite safe from this degree of absurdity, but we are mistaken. If a man watches his own mind, I believe he will find that what profess to be specially advanced or philosophic conceptions of God are, in his thinking, always accompanied by vague images which, if inspected, would turn out to be even more absurd than the man-like images aroused by Christian theology.[3]

Our conceptions of God are determined by the images through which his revelation appears. Finite beings in a finite realm have no *absolute* knowledge of the infinite God, only analogies, models, symbols and abstractions. "We cannot see light, though by light we can see things," Lewis reminds us. "Statements about God are extrapolations from knowledge of other things which the divine illumination enables us to know."[4]

One of the ways that "divine illumination" enables us to know certain things about God is through what Lewis calls *myth*—the primary mode of imagery, the highest form of symbolism.

MYTH CONVEYS THE INEXPRESSIBLE

Aslan, Lewis's mythopoeic deity in his Narnian tales, is not a tame lion. His nature cannot be contained in abstract thought or adequately expressed in theological language. But by getting to know the imaginary Aslan as we read of his activities in Narnia, we begin to perceive what God must be like. In the contemplation of such mythic images, Lewis believes, "we come nearest to experiencing as a concrete what can otherwise be understood only as an abstraction."[5]

Myth, of course, does not mean falsehood! It may or may not be based on historical facts but in essence is truer than history or fact. What Ransom discovered when he traveled to Perelandra was "that the triple distinction of truth from myth and both from fact was purely terrestrial." [6] Because the term *myth* often connotes untruth, Lewis was tempted not to use it: "I must either use the word *myth* or coin a word, and I think the former the lesser evil of the two." [7] Lewis uses the term in the Socratic sense, "an account of what *may have been* the historical fact." This is "not to be confused with 'myth' in Dr. Niebuhr's sense (*i.e.*, a symbolic representation of non-historical truth)." [8]

Myth, as Lewis conceives it, is an archetypal tale which reflects, portrays, and signifies eternal realities. Myth is a "real though unfocussed gleam of divine truth falling on human imagination" which enables the inexpressible to be conveyed.[9] Myth, as the highest form of symbolism, reaches after "some transcendental reality which the forms of discursive thought cannot contain." [10] Not that myth is irrational; rather it is non-rational. Reality is infinitely greater than human rational conception.

Humphrey Carpenter, author of the authorized biography on J. R. R. Tolkien, recounts (on p. 147) a significant conversation between Lewis and Tolkien which occurred in September 1931. Lewis had become a theist by this time, though not yet a Christian, and was troubled about the relationship between myth and fact.

"Myths are lies," Lewis claimed, "even though lies breathed through silver."

Tolkien tried to explain to his friend the truth of myth. Pointing to the great trees of Magdalen Grove where they were having their discussion that evening, Tolkien said:

"You call a tree a tree . . . and you think nothing more of the word. But it was not a 'tree' until someone gave it that name. You call a star a star, and say it is just a ball of matter moving on a mathematical course. But that is merely how *you* see it. By so naming things and describing them you are only inventing your own terms about them. And just as speech is invention about objects and ideas, so myth is invention about truth."

When divine truth falls on human imagination, myth is born. It is like seeing a glimpse of reality without the hindrance of concrete facts or abstract data. Myth is the father of abstraction and concrete particulars. Far from being less than true or factual, myth puts us in touch with Reality in a more intimate way than by knowing what is merely true or factual. Myth, according to Lewis, is the best means of divine communication.

In defining what he means by myth, Lewis identifies at least six significant characteristics: myth (1) can be distinguished from allegory, (2) is fundamentally extraliteral, (3) has elements of fantasy, (4) embodies universal Reality, (5) has a unifying effect on the receiver, (6) functions as a bridge between worlds.

Myth Can Be Distinguished from Allegory

Lewis employed allegory in writing *The Pilgrim's Regress* and *The Great Divorce.* His space trilogy, his children's stories, and his adult fiction, *Till We Have Faces,* however, are more properly called myths, though they contain allegorical elements. The difference between the two forms of symbolism is significant.

In traditional allegory, there is a rough one-to-one correspondence between the symbol and that which is signified. Cupid represents erotic love, for example, and Bunyan's Giant, despair. When you begin with an immaterial concept (e.g., despair) and create a material personification to make its meaning clear, you are using allegory. But if you reverse this process and begin with the material (e.g., a lion) to symbolize what is immaterial, you employ metaphor or myth. In allegory, the images stand for concepts; in myth, they symbolize an imagined *something* which cannot be reduced to a concept. Allegory can always be translated back into meaningful concepts; mythical meaning cannot be stated in conceptual terms. Allegory is clear and unambiguous; myth is more complex: it creates a world of its own where reality is free to reveal itself in terms of that particular world and applies to many levels of meaning.

Myth Is Fundamentally Extraliterary

Only in a limited sense is myth an expanded metaphor. Fundamentally, myth does not exist in words at all, and can be distinguished from the language structures in which it is expressed. Literary myths (tales embodied in literature) are at least twice removed from the Reality to which they point. Primary myths (legends, stories, plots and patterns which have meaning independent of their medium) are only one step removed.

Consider the myth of Orpheus, roughly outlined by Lewis in *An Experiment in Criticism:*

> There was a man who sang and played the harp so well that even beasts and trees crowded to hear him. And when his wife died he went down alive into the land of the dead and made music before the King of the Dead till even he had compassion and gave him back his wife, on condition that he lead her up out of that land without once looking back to see her until they came out into the light. But when they were nearly out, one moment too soon, the man looked back, and she vanished from him forever.[11]

The tale itself strikes deep and affects our very being. "The fact that Virgil and others have told it in good poetry is irrelevant," Lewis declares. "It is true that such a story can hardly reach us except in words. But this is logically accidental. If some perfected art of mime or silent film or serial pictures could make it clear with no words at all, it would still affect us in the same way."[12] Thus myth, in its primary state, is extraliterary.

Myth Has Elements of Fantasy

Though myth is primarily a pattern of events and only secondarily a series of words, the nature of the tale is always fantastic—it deals with apparent impossibilities and preternaturals.

Fantasy is perhaps best defined as a pleasing imaginary construction in which human experience and spiritual reality assume clarity and universal significance. A fantasy is a fairytale of sorts which says by implication, "I am merely a work of art. You must take me as such—must enjoy me for my suggestions, my beauty, my irony, my construction, and so forth. There is no question of anything like this happening to you in the real world." [13] Particular examples of fantasy in the world of litera- ture would include, "The Rime of the Ancient Mariner," *Gulliver's Travels, The Wind in the Willows,* and of course, selected works by George MacDonald, Charles Williams, J. R. R. Tolkien, and C. S. Lewis.

The fantasy element of myth is essential to its nature and function. Unfortunately, not everybody can be inspired by the truth revealed through an imaginary construction. Lewis's tales of Narnia, for example, have meaning not to those who insist on literal truth but to those who have spiritual eyes to see and ears to hear the truth conveyed through myth.

Myth Embodies Universal Reality

The greatest myths, according to Lewis, imaginatively em- body universal realities. By perceiving what myth represents, universal principles can be derived. The actual Reality of which myth is only an image is always greater than the abstract mean- ing derived. The moment we try to state the truth embodied in myth in conceptional-verbal form, we get abstraction. "It is only while receiving the myth as a story that you experience the [universal] principle concretely," Lewis says.[14]

The story of Job in the Bible, for example, though it may be based on historical fact, contains more universal truth as myth than can possibly be stated in any purely literal understanding. The same can be said of the story of Jonah, the account of the Fall, or the visions in the Book of Revelation. The Reality em- bodied in myth cannot be adequately defined, put into words, or grasped by the intellect. It must be imagined or experienced.

While myths help us experience Ultimate Reality, we must not expect too much from them. Myths are only shadows of the light of God. We walk in the light by faith, not by sight or exhaustive understanding.

Myth Has a Unifying Effect on the Receiver

The effect of myth is one of awe, enchantment, and inspiration. Myth evokes powerful emotional responses which have a unifying effect on the receiver. In the contemplation of mythic images, one's consciousness is enlarged, enabling apprehension of new meaning and insight. Myth's effect is essentially poetic vision. Reality is received through the imaginative embrace of pictorial patterns made romantically and spiritually real.

Is it any wonder, then, that the Adam and Eve story and other biblical narrations, rich in mythic meaning and spiritual truth, affect us so profoundly? The images evoked through myth register beneath the surface of the mind, allowing us to actually experience Reality and grasp eternal truths which might baffle the intellect and confuse the mind.

Through the mythic qualities of the historical story of Joseph and his brothers, for example, we are able to feel (or intuit) the unifying truth of both fate and free will. "What you intended for evil, God meant for good," Joseph told his brothers who betrayed him. Thus God's sovereignty and man's responsibility are not mutually exclusive ideas. Myth enables us to synthesize what discursive reason would show to be contradictory.

Again, consider the interplay of fate and free will in Lewis's science fiction novel, *Perelandra*. The philologist Ransom was chosen to do an impossible task: to destroy the powerful Unman on the infiltrated planet Venus. After an exhausting struggle with his own passions over whether he was capable of such a task, or even desired to attempt it, he finally realized that "the thing was going to be done" whether or not he chose to do it.

Was Ransom predestined to destroy the Un-man? Did he exercise free will? Lewis allows the truth to unfold mythically:

> You might say, if you liked, that the power of choice had been simply set aside and an inflexible destiny substituted for it. On the other hand, you might say that he had been delivered from the rhetoric of his passions and had emerged into unassailable freedom. Ransom could not, for the life of him, see any difference between these two statements. Predestination and freedom were

apparently identical. He could no longer see any meaning in the many arguments he had heard on this subject.[15]

To feel the truth of both fate and free will is something not obtained from rational arguments on the subject. It is something one can intuitively perceive in something like the story of Joseph or of Ransom. It can also be directly experienced in a moment of mystical encounter with God.

The climax of mythic perception is indeed a romantic-mystical experience. Myth is capable of arousing in us, according to Lewis,

> sensations we have never had before, never anticipated having, as though we had broken out of our normal mode of consciousness and "possessed joys not promised to our birth." It gets under our skin, hits us at a level deeper than our thoughts or even our passions, troubles oldest certainties till all questions are re-opened, and in general shocks us more fully awake than we are for most of our lives.[16]

Myth Functions as a Bridge between the Worlds

Myth functions as a bridge between the infinite realm of Absolute Reality and the finite realm of abstract, propositional truth. As Lewis describes it metaphorically, "Myth is the mountain whence all the different streams arise which become truths down here in the valley; *in hac valle abstractionis* [in this valley of separation]. Or, if you prefer, myth is the isthmus which connects the peninsular world of thought with that vast continent we really belong to." [17]

The bridge-building function of myth is illustrated by Lewis in the fairytale *The Voyage of the Dawn Treader,* in a conversation between Caspian, prince of Narnia, and his English guests: " 'Do you mean to say,' asked Caspian [who ruled inhabitants of a flat world], 'that you three came from a round world (round like a ball). . . ! We have fairy-tales in which there are round worlds and I always loved them. I never believed there were any real ones. But I've always wished there were and I've always longed to live in one.' " [18] Caspian's flat world and the round world of the three children stand in the same relation as our natural world and the supernatural realm depicted in fantasy. We, too, have fairytales or myths which point to supernatural dimensions of reality. By embracing myth we gain a vision of the transcendent realm where we, like Caspian, have always longed to live.

In *The Last Battle,* all the Narnian myths and visions of the transcendent realm are finally realized. "I have come home at last!" shouts the Unicorn with joy. "This is my real country." [19] Professor Digory tries to explain to the children the platonic nature of the New Narnia which had finally replaced the old:

> "When Aslan said you could never go back to Narnia, he meant the Narnia you were thinking of. But that was not the real Narnia. That had a beginning and an end. It was only a shadow or a copy of the real Narnia which has always been here and always will be here: just as our own world, England and all, is only a shadow or copy of something in Aslan's real world. You need not mourn over Narnia, Lucy. All of the old Narnia that mattered, all the dear creatures, have been drawn into the real Narnia through the Door. And of course it is different; as different as a real thing is from a shadow or as waking life is from a dream. . . . It's all in Plato, all in Plato: bless me, what *do* they teach them at these schools!" [20]

Wishful Thinking or the Truly Real?

Lewis's approach to myth, revelation and Scripture presupposes the validity of Platonic Idealism. Not that he presumed the geographic necessity of a "two-story universe"; rather he perceived, metaphorically, a unified Reality where the "natural" and the "supernatural" realms "co-inhere." [21] Assuming Plato and Lewis are correct in affirming the existence of the two realms of Reality, then how are the universals transposed into the particulars?

In his essay, "Transposition," Lewis answers this question by explaining that when a higher dimension descends into a lower one, it is like translating from a language which has a large vocabulary into one that has a small vocabulary. Or, to use another analogy, transposition can be compared to the problems involved in drawing. How can aspects of a three-dimensional world be represented on a two-dimensional sheet of paper? Obviously something will be lost in the conversion. The relationship between the higher realm and its transposition in the lower is likewise abstract. The correspondence between the universals and particulars is not exact or absolute but rather symbolic or sacramental. The thing signified descends in substance so that the lower partakes of the higher as the higher reproduces itself, imperfectly, in the lower.[22]

An example of transposition is the Incarnation. God—the infinite, inscrutable, indescribable, "wholly other"—transcending the universe, took on human form to reveal himself to man. In so doing, the Creator said in effect, "My children, I want you to see and experience My eternal essence in the form of a finite particular." Thus Christ became "the visible likeness of the invisible God." Yet God in essence is more than his particular manifestation as Son. God reveals himself in other forms as well, namely, Father and Spirit.

The same is true in other aspects of divine revelation. When eternal realities are transposed into our finite realm, something is lost in the translation. A divine concession is made. There is a deficiency of substance when Eternal Truth takes on finite form. The particulars we see and affirm as true are only shadows of the truly Real. The higher realm of Ultimate Reality can only be seen "through a glass darkly," only "known in part."

There are two basic approaches to transposition, according to Lewis. If we interpret the world of universals in terms of the particulars, as Aristotle did, we are tempted to conclude that the so-called higher or spiritual realm is derived from the lower or physical realm. If the natural is all that exists, then the supposed supernatural is merely a projection or imaginary extension of the natural. If this be the case, man's highest values are simply illusions and we are guilty of what Freud called "wish-fulfillment." This is what confused John in *The Pilgrim's Regress*:

> "How do you know that there is no such place as my Island?"
> "Do you wish very much that there was?"

"I do."

"Have you never before imagined anything to be true because you greatly wished for it?"

John thought for a little, and then he said, "Yes."

"And your Island is *like* an imagination—isn't it?"

"I suppose so."

"It is just the sort of thing you *would* imagine merely through wanting it—the whole thing is very suspicious." [23]

But if we approach transposition from *above*, we then perceive with Plato that the natural is a dim reflection of a supernatural realm. Life indeed has meaning and significance, for the values and visions we hold dear are from a spiritual source outside ourselves and the particulars of nature.

Although there are always naturalistic explanations for those experiences which faith claims are from above, Christians approach the phenomenon of transposition "from inside," as Lewis so confidently asserts. "With whatever sense of unworthiness, with whatever sense of audacity, we must affirm that we know a little of the higher system which is being transposed." [24]

"Spiritual things are spiritually discerned," Lewis states. "He that is spiritual judgeth all things," said the Apostle Paul. Plato, perhaps, expressed it best of all:

". . . Whose light would you say it is that makes our eyes see and objects be seen most perfectly?"

". . . you mean the sun, of course. . . ."

"Apply the analogy to the mind. When the mind's eye is fixed on objects illuminated by truth and reality, it understands and knows them, and its possession of intelligence is evident; but when it is fixed on the twilight world of change and decay, it can only form opinions, its vision is confused and its opinions shifting. . . . Then what gives the objects of knowledge their truth and the knower's mind the power of knowing is the form of the good." [25]

God's Revelation Assumes Different Forms

If God takes the initiative in transposition, then what are some of the ways he reveals himself to man? In *Mere Chris-*

tianity, Lewis identifies four means of divine disclosure: conscience (or "The Universal Ought"), the chosen people of Israel (or "Election"), pagan mythology (or "Good Dreams"), the Christ event (or "Incarnation"). In *The Problem of Pain* he adds two more to the list: Immortal longing (or *"Sehnsucht"*), and the Idea of the Holy (or "The Experience of the Numinous").

The Experience of the Numinous: God's Holiness

Influenced by Rudolf Otto's *The Idea of the Holy,* Lewis refers to man's basic awareness of the Divine (or the Holy) as "the experience of the Numinous." [26] From ancient times, man believed the universe to be "haunted" by the supernatural or the Numinous, as evidenced throughout literature and human experience. Sensing the terrifying presence of the Holy, man could but fall to the ground, hide his face in shame, and echo the words of the prophet Isaiah: "Woe is me! for I am undone; because I am a man of unclean lips, and I dwell in the midst of a people of unclean lips" (Isa. 6:5).

Fallen and finite humanity has cause to shrink in the presence of divine goodness. Separated from that which was his original nature, man feels utterly sinful and corrupt. It is with combined awe and fear that one encounters the Numinous, as Orual did in *Till We Have Faces.* Ashamed and afraid, she later pondered the question, "Why must holy places be dark places?" [27] In *Perelandra* Lewis, as a character in the novel, is portrayed in the awful presence of the Numinous, visibly shaken, fearful, and "undone":

> My sensations were, it is true, in some ways very unpleasant. The fact that it was quite obviously not organic—the knowledge that intelligence was somehow located in this homogeneous cylinder of light but not related to it as our consciousness is related to our brains and nerves—was profoundly disturbing. It would not fit into our categories. The response which we ordinarily make to a living creature and that which one makes to an inanimate object were here both equally inappropriate. . . . I felt sure that the creature was what we call "good," but I wasn't sure whether I

liked "goodness" so much as I had supposed. This is a very terrible experience. As long as what you are afraid of is something evil, you may still hope that the good may come to your rescue. But suppose you struggle through to the good and find that it also is dreadful? . . . Here at last was a bit of that world from beyond the world, which I had always supposed that I loved and desired, breaking through and appearing to my senses: and I didn't like it, I wanted it to go away. I wanted every possible distance, gulf, curtain, blanket, and barrier to be placed between it and me.[28]

We love God but we also fear him. We are but dust compared to his greatness, filthy rags to his holiness. Through the experience of the Numinous, God manifests himself.

The Universal Ought: Cosmic Bluff or Moral Responsibility?

Another medium of revelation is conscience—the universal recognition of the *Tao*, or the Moral Law. As developed by Lewis in *Mere Christianity*, whenever people quarrel, make excuses for their behavior, or blame others, they are assuming an objective, universal value system of fair play or decent behavior. This universal sense of "ought," as Lewis calls it in *The Abolition of Man*, is either morally binding, entailing adverse consequences if violated, or else nothing more (or less) than a cosmic bluff. If the latter, then there is no moral reason for acknowledging any values save those which seem personally expedient or which might yield the greatest pleasure. If the former, man is responsible for his behavior.

The fact is that most people are not inclined to regard as a bluff their sense of right and wrong. Moral responsibility appears to be universally acknowledged. In every culture, Lewis observes, individuals feel toward certain proposed actions "the experiences expressed by the words 'I ought' or 'I ought not.' "[29] Though not all agree on the exact content of the Moral Law, most people affirm that one ought to behave morally. Differences in moral perspective may exist, yet they never amount "to anything like a total difference."[30] Given the minor variation of morality among cultures, "all men stand condemned," declares Lewis, "not by alien codes of ethics, but by their own."[31]

Moral awareness naturally leads to religious consciousness, as Lewis goes on to explain: "When the Numinous Power of which [men] feel awe is made the guardian of the morality to which they feel obligation," religion emerges. Virtually all cultures and societies have made this essential connection between conscience (or moral awareness) and the source of their morality, as the Apostle Paul recognizes: "For what can be known about God is made plain to them, because God has shown it to them. Ever since the creation of the world his invisible nature, namely his eternal power and deity, has been clearly perceived in the things that have been made. So they are without excuse" (Rom. 1:19–20). "When the Gentiles who have not the law do by nature what the law requires, they are a law to themselves, even though they do not have the law. They show that what the law requires is written on their hearts, while their conscience also bears witness and their conflicting thoughts accuse or perhaps excuse them" (Rom. 2:14–16).

Sehnsucht: *The Hound of Heaven*

In his chapter on heaven in *The Problem of Pain*, Lewis defines yet another fundamental medium of divine revelation. *Sehnsucht*, or immortal longing—the central motif of romanticism—can be recognized in nearly all of Lewis's works, yet perhaps is described most concisely in *Mere Christianity*:

Most people, if they had really learned to look into their own hearts, would know that they do want, and want acutely, something that cannot be had in this world. There are all sorts of things in this world that offer to give it to you, but they never quite keep their promise. The longings which arise in us when we first fall in love, or first think of some foreign country, or first take up some subject that excites us, are longings which no marriage, no travel, no learning, can really satisfy.

Sehnsucht is that mysterious something we all want, we all grasp at, "in the first moment of longing, which just fades away in the reality." Its purpose in human experience, according to Lewis, is to point us to the Source of our desire. "If I find in myself a desire which no experience in this world can satisfy, the most probable explanation is that I was made for another world. If none of my earthly pleasures satisfy it, that does not prove that the universe is a fraud. Probably earthly pleasures were never meant to satisfy it, but only to arouse it, to suggest the real thing." [32]

The fact that the best of life's pleasures are really only half-pleasures, compared to the imagined ideal, is God's way of giving us a taste of what heaven is like, a thirst for our true home. *Sehnsucht*, as Corbin Scott Carnell personifies it, is "the hound of heaven, relentlessly pursuing man that he may discover his true identity and home." [33] (A more detailed study of *Sehnsucht* in Lewis's romantic theology is provided in the Appendix.)

Election: Israel and the Law

"[God] selected one particular people and spent several centuries hammering into their heads the sort of God He was," Lewis writes in *Mere Christianity*. "Those people were the Jews, and the Old Testament gives an account of the hammering process." [34] God acted redemptively in the history of Israel, revealed himself through prophet and priest, miraculously intervened in the life of the community, and sought to teach them his ways so that the world through them might be blessed.

In *The Pilgrim's Regress*, Lewis develops this theme—that God revealed himself to Israel, "the Shepherd People," through the Law. But the "Landlord has circulated other things besides the Rules," John learns on his journey. "What use are Rules to people who cannot read?" For the illiterate (or the Pagans), God reveals himself in "pictures" or myths. Because these myths contained a Divine call, many pagans saw glimpses of God.

Both the Shepherds with their "Rules" and the Pagans with their "pictures," however, were incomplete in themselves, as Lewis explains: "The truth is that a Shepherd is only a half a man, and a Pagan is only half a man, so that neither people was well without the other, nor could either be healed until the Landlord's Son came into the country." [35]

In both cultures, Hebrew and pagan, revelation was gradual,

culminating finally in the historic Incarnation. The notion of progressive revelation suggests that God discloses himself to man in a way that is best suited to man's particular stage of religious development. For pagan culture, divine revelation took the form of mythology. For the Hebrew culture, God spoke through the Law and the prophets. Christianity is the grand culmination of progressive revelation and religious maturity in both cultures.

Good Dreams: Pagan Premonitions of Christ

Pagan myths or "good dreams," as Lewis refers to them in *Mere Christianity,* comprise yet another medium of divine revelation. Scattered throughout human history are archetypal patterns, stories, rituals, and religious motifs "about a god who dies and comes to life again and, by his death, has somehow given new life to men." [36]

In *Reflections on the Psalms,* Lewis cites a passage from the Roman poet Virgil (70–19 B.C.), who wrote in one of his Eclogues: "The great procession of the ages begins anew. Now the Virgin returns, the reign of Saturn returns, and the new child is sent down from heaven." The "reign of Saturn," Lewis reminds us, is the great Roman age that roughly corresponds to the Garden of Eden before the Fall in Hebrew mythology. Virgil's poem describes the new paradisal age which would emerge with this nativity. Apparently, Lewis surmises, some dim prophetic knowledge of Christ's birth impressed the mind of the famous pagan poet.[37]

Plato was another, perhaps the greatest of all myth-makers. In his *Republic,* we are asked to imagine a perfectly righteous man, who "will be scourged, tortured, and imprisoned, his eyes will be put out, and after enduring every humiliation he will be crucified. . . ." [38] Although Plato was clearly inspired by the death of Socrates, he is really depicting, according to Lewis, "the fate of goodness in a wicked and misunderstanding world." The obvious similarity between Plato's vision and the Passion of Christ was not one of coincidence but insight. "It is the very same thing of which that Passion is the supreme illustration." [39]

"And what are we to say of those gods in various Pagan mythologies who are killed and rise again and who thereby renew or transform the life of their worshippers or of nature?" [40] Lewis asks in *Reflections on the Psalms,* referring to the corn-kings in the nature religions who personify the annual death and resurrection of corn. He asks again, "Can one believe there was just *nothing* in that persistent *motif* of blood, death, and resurrection, which runs like a black and scarlet cord through all the greater myths—through Balder and Dionysus and Adonis and the Grail too?" [41]

How are Christians to understand the obvious similarities between pagan myths and Christianity? Either pagan mythology is essentially demonic and functions as counterfeit revelation for the purpose of confusing mankind, or else it is the dim foreshadowing of God's supreme revelation in Christ. Lewis identifies with the latter view: "Surely the history of the human mind hangs together better if you suppose that all this was the first shadowy approach of something whose reality came with Christ." [42]

The difference between pagan myths of redemption and the Divine Incarnation in history "is not the difference between falsehood and truth. It is the difference between a real event on the one hand and dim dreams or premonitions of that same event on the other." [43] As Lewis explains in *Miracles,* Christ is like the corn-kings of pagan mythology "because the Corn-King is a portrait of Him. The similarity is not in the least unreal or accidental. For the Corn-King is derived (through human imagination) from the facts of Nature, and the facts of Nature from her Creator; the Death and Re-birth pattern is in her because it was first in Him." [44]

This archetypal pattern of redemption—birth, death, new life —is "a thing written all over the world." [45] Embedded in the natural processes of the sun rising and setting, the cycles of the seasons, the cycle of life, or a seed being planted in the ground and dying only to live again is the mythological truth that man must die to live: "In the sequence of night and day, in the annual death and rebirth of the crops, in the myths which these

processes gave rise to, in the strong, if half-articulate, feeling
. . . that man himself must undergo some sort of death if he
would truly live, there is already a likeness permitted by God
to that truth on which all depends." [46] One of the functions of
the natural world, it seems, is to furnish symbols that point to
spiritual reality. Nature supplies the substance for myth; God
supplies the meaning.

Incarnation: Myth Become Fact

Though God sprinkled his revelation throughout the natural
world in various forms, supreme revelation had to come through
historical fact, Lewis asserts. The truth first appeared in mythical form, "and then by a long process of condensing or focussing
finally becomes incarnate as History." [47] In the historical incarnation, he explains, myth became fact: "There was a man
born among these Jews who claimed to be . . . 'one with' the
Something which is at once the awful haunter of nature and the
giver of the moral law." [48]

As a young, atheistic intellectual, Lewis's major stumbling
block to accepting Christianity was the fact that the Christian
religion did not seem to offer anything new. His knowledge of
the life, death, and resurrection theme in other religions convinced him that Christianity was anything but unique. But
eventually Lewis was able to see that ancient religious myths
converged and found their fulfillment in the Christ event:

> The question was no longer to find the one simply true religion
> among a thousand religions simply false. It was rather, "Where
> has religion reached its true maturity? Where, if anywhere, have
> the hints of all Paganism been fulfilled?" With the irreligious I
> was no longer concerned; their view of life was henceforth out of
> court. As against them, the whole mass of those who had wor-
> shiped—all who had danced and sung and sacrificed and
> trembled and adored—were clearly right. [49]

All the pagan myths were merely premonitions of "Nature's
Original," as Lewis calls Christ. [50] When the Word became flesh,
when God became man in Jesus Christ, the process of myth
was actualized and revelation was complete. Pagan myths, mo-

tifs, and rituals were noble yet inadequate vehicles of divine revelation—distorted reflections of the real thing. But in the Christ event, Lewis explains in his essay, "Myth Became Fact," "we pass from a Balder or Osiris, dying nobody knows when or where, to a historical Person crucified . . . under Pontius Pilate." God's progressive revelation, which appeared only faintly in the great myths, had culminated in historic fact.

"The heart of Christianity is a myth which is also a fact," Lewis insists in this essay. "The old myth of the Dying God, *without ceasing to be myth*, comes down from the heaven of legend and imagination to the earth of history." When the Word became flesh, all the properties of myth were carried with him into the world of fact.

"To be truly Christian," Lewis admonishes, "we must both assent to the historical fact and also receive the myth (fact though it has become) with the same imaginative embrace we accord to all myths." Intuition is needed to grasp the meaning of the Incarnation. Its reality is greater than what we can understand by our intellect alone. The Christian myth addresses our imagination and requires an imaginative response. In scriptural terms, the Holy Spirit is necessary to interpret revelation and impress God's eternal truth upon our hearts. A man who doubted the Christian story as fact "but continually fed on it as myth would, perhaps, be more spiritually alive than one who assented and did not think much about it," he surmises. But it is necessary to believe both. Incarnation is a grand synthesis of myth and fact, says Lewis, "for this is the marriage of heaven and earth: Perfect Myth and Perfect Fact: claiming not only our love and our obedience, but also our wonder and delight, addressed to the savage, the child, and the poet in each one of us no less than to the moralist, the scholar, and the philosopher." [51]

It can be concluded at this point that Scripture for Lewis functions as myth, as well as historic fact. It has most of the qualities of imaginative literature and all the characteristics of myth, requiring an imaginative embrace to perceive meaning.

Myth, it must be remembered, does not mean lie, error, illusion or misunderstood history. The term has little to do with fact or history but transcends both. Properly understood, myth is a medium of divine revelation bringing a level of understanding superseding that which can be known through facts and history. To regard a portion of Scripture as myth, far from being less than true, is to acknowledge a higher truth and a deeper reality than could otherwise be expressed. As the Voice says to John in *The Pilgrim's Regress,* myth is "the veil under which I have chosen to appear even from the first until now." The value of myth, of course, depends on the receiver. One must use imaginative faith to embrace myth's meaning. "For this end I made your senses and for this end your imagination, that you might see My face and live." [52]

SCRIPTURE AS INSPIRED LITERATURE

"In what way is the Bible inspired?" was the question raised in chapter 1. To agree with Lewis would be to answer "mythically." Unfortunately, the popular conception of the term *myth* is far from Lewis's understanding. It would be better to use a different term.

"Literary inspiration" is a useful phrase to denote Lewis's view of Scripture. The Bible is to be approached as inspired literature. Its literary elements—images, symbols, myths and metaphors—are actual *embodiments* of spiritual reality, *vehicles* of divine revelation.

To appreciate a particular passage of Scripture in a literary way is not to dismiss its significance in truth and value, as Lewis explains,

Some people when they say that a thing is meant "metaphorically" conclude from this that it is hardly meant at all. They rightly think that Christ spoke metaphorically when he told us to carry the cross: they wrongly conclude that carrying the cross means nothing more than leading a respectable life and subscribing moderately to charities. They reasonably think that hell "fire" is a metaphor—and unwisely conclude that it means nothing more serious than remorse. They say that the story of the Fall in

Genesis is not literal; and then go on to say . . . that it was really a fall upwards—which is like saying that because "My heart is broken" contains a metaphor, it therefore means "I feel very cheerful." This mode of interpretation I regard, frankly, as nonsense. For me the Christian doctrines which are "metaphorical"—or which have become metaphorical with the increase of abstract thought—mean something which is just as "supernatural" or shocking after we have removed the ancient imagery as it was before.[53]

Scripture characteristically portrays a nonstatic God acting in wrath or pity, being jealous or pleased, hearing and answering prayers of faith. Lewis admits that all such language is metaphorical. "But when we say that, we must not smuggle in the idea that we can throw the analogy away and, as it were, get in behind it to a purely literal truth. All we can really substitute for the analogical expression is some theological abstraction."[54]

Likewise, says Lewis, when we speak of "seeing" or "meeting" God "face to face" we are speaking anthropomorphically, for God in reality is within, above, below and all about us. Metaphoric language must be balanced by metaphysical and theological abstractions. "While anthropomorphic images are a concession" to our finite understanding, Lewis adds, let us not think that the abstractions are any closer to the truth. "Both are equally concessions; each singly misleading, and the two together mutually corrective."[55]

Conscious of both the literary nature of Scripture and the potential danger of some readers failing to fully appreciate what to them is "merely metaphoric," Lewis offers two suggestions for biblical exegetics: "(1) Never take the images literally. (2) When the *purport* of the images—what they say to our fear and hope and will and affections—seems to conflict with the theological abstractions, trust the purport of the images every time."[56]

The best example of proper exegetics is accepting at face value the countless biblical metaphors for God: Creator, Redeemer, Lamb of God, High Priest, Star out of Jacob, Good Shepherd, Suffering Servant, Prince of Peace, Man of Sorrows, Wisdom, Providence, Beloved, Everlasting Father, Anchor of

Faith, Branch, Vine, Bread, Living Water, the Door, the Way, King of the Jews, Son of Righteousness, King of Kings and Lord of Lords, Alpha and Omega, Son of Man, Son of God, Only Begotten Son, Ascended Lord, Perfect Righteousness, First-fruits, the Word, Savior, Love, Life, Truth, Rose of Sharon, Author and Finisher of our Faith. . . . To discard such rich and meaningful literary images and replace them with abstract theological statements about the nature of God is to fail to appreciate the purport of Scripture.

Lewis, like Rudolf Bultmann, insists that the literary elements of Scripture be recognized. He differs from the neoorthodox theologian, however, in asserting that the literary medium can be distinguished but not divorced from the inspired message. If divine revelation comes through the purport of the images, then Bultmann's demythologizing efforts are really a remythologizing of Scripture, and the "substituting a poorer mythology for a richer." [57]

The Bible as inspired literature requires *good reading* and *intuitive perception*. To appreciate Scripture, as with great literature, we must begin by receiving the text *in the way it was intended*. If the story of Adam and Eve possesses mythic qualities, it should be received with an imaginative embrace whether or not it was also historical. If the miracles of Jesus, as Lewis believes, are recorded as historical occurrences, they are not to be spiritualized away.

"Where, then, do we draw the line between explaining and 'explaining away'?" Lewis asks in his essay "Horrid Red Things." He did not think the task too difficult, as he goes on to say:

"All that concerns the un-incarnate activities of God—His operation on that plane of being where sense cannot enter— must be taken along with imagery which we know to be, in the literal sense, untrue. But there can be no defense for applying the same treatment to the miracles of the Incarnate God. They are recorded as events on this earth which affected human senses. They are the sort of thing we can describe literally. If Christ turned water into wine, and we had been present, we could have seen, smelled, and tasted. The story that He did so is not of the same order as His 'sitting at the right hand of the Father.' It is either fact, or legend, or lie. You must take it or leave it." [58]

The literary interpretation of Scripture, like myth, is somewhat subjective. Its value depends on the one who receives God's Word from its pages. Like all great literature, the Bible has several levels of meaning and can meet the individual where he is. To understand Scripture, we should look beyond the language to what is represented, thereby gaining intuitive insight into the nature of reality. We respond not to the Bible per se but to the realities conveyed through the Bible by the power of the Holy Spirit who leads us into all truth. By thus distinguishing the literary medium from the divine message, God's Word can more clearly be heard.

We have examined Lewis's peculiar blend of liberal-conservative theology, neoplatonic epistemology, romantic approach to literature, metaphorical analysis of language, and literary understanding of myth, revelation and Scripture. We are now ready to interpret his thoughts on the nature of biblical inspiration and relate them to the present controversy over inerrancy.

—5—

The Question of Inerrancy

The very *kind* of truth we are often demanding [of
Scripture] was, in my opinion, never even envisaged by
the ancients.

—Letter from Lewis, May 7, 1959 [1]

Lewis is certainly no twentieth-century Plato, Aristotle, or even
Aquinas, though he has much in common with his ancient
teachers. Neither is he a credentialed philosopher or theologian.
In an age which rewards originality above all, he offers no new
religious theory or political ideology. His unique contribution is
in giving fresh and fluid expression to old ideas. In trying to be
unoriginal, Lewis ironically succeeds in being original, just as
others who seek so desperately at originality fail.

In Lewis we find a certain reluctance to systematize his im-
pressions of reality. He prefers rather to embrace the mysteries
of religion with intuitive faith. On the broad essentials of
Christianity (e.g., God's existence, Christ's divinity, man's immortality, sin's reality and remedy), Lewis with his characteristic
either/or logic argues dogmatically. On doctrinal details, however, he is unassuming and tolerant. Often he confesses to
ignorance or to living in the tension of two conflicting points of
view. When he does offer an opinion on a particular controversy
he is careful to preface his remarks by stating that they are only
his "tentative thoughts," that he may, in fact, be wrong. After

all, *savoir* (abstract knowledge *about* Reality) has only a functional value in this life. "If anything is useful to you," Lewis says of his theological explanations, "use it; if anything is not, never give it a second thought." [2]

It is in this spirit that Lewis offers his thoughts on the nature of biblical inspiration and the question of inerrancy, which has been the subject of this study. In a similar spirit I now will offer my interpretation of C. S. Lewis on Scripture. Thus far I have attempted simply to identify Lewis's basic assumptions and, to the best of my ability, faithfully present his religious views as they relate to his understanding of Scripture. Now I will try to draw conclusions and offer an interpretation which should be distinguished from my attempted objective presentation of Lewis's thoughts.

I will begin by offering a brief historic sketch of the development of biblical inspiration as a Christian doctrine, commenting on how Lewis might respond to the various traditional approaches. The concluding chapter will be an attempt to state clearly my interpretation of Lewis's view of Scripture.

What Did the Early Church Believe?

The question of biblical inspiration, like many Christian doctrines, has never been completely resolved within the church. Men of faith have struggled with the question through the ages, advanced many theories, and held countless views.

The emphasis of the early church fathers was on the question of canonicity, not the meaning of inspiration. That Scripture was inspired and authoritative was a position universally accepted by Christians, yet the question of inerrancy commanded little attention. Clement of Alexandria (150?–215?) believed that all Scripture had been spoken by the mouth of the Lord, while Origen (185?–254?) declared that some passages in the Bible "are not literally true but absurd and impossible." In the fifth century Augustine (354–430) championed the cause of biblical orthodoxy, yet cautioned against literalism: "We must be on guard against giving interpretations of Scripture that are far-fetched or opposed to science, and so exposing the Word of God to the ridicule of unbelievers."

The early church, it would appear, required less of Scripture (in terms of inerrancy) than the church requires today. The kind of truth we demand of the Bible was in Lewis's view, "never even envisaged by the ancients."

What Did the Medieval Church Believe?

In the Middle Ages, the authority of the church took precedence over the teachings of the Bible. During the Scholastic period, Christians were relatively silent on the question of inspiration, being far more concerned with the status of the Bible in relation to other authorities. Peter Abelard (1079–1142) expressed doubts as to the total accuracy of Scripture from a historical standpoint. Thomas Aquinas (1225?–74) found a place for the human element in Scripture. Generally speaking, however, the church of the Middle Ages affirmed the authority of Scripture *through* the church in matters of faith and practice.

What Did the Reformers Assert about Scripture?

The Reformers dared to assert that the medieval church had distorted biblical revelation. They rallied around the cry of *Sola Scriptura*—"Scripture only" as the measure of faith. When what the Bible taught conflicted with what the church taught, the biblical authority was to be trusted as God's Word.

John Calvin (1509–64) often spoke of God as the author of the Bible, and the canon of Scripture as God's gift to the church. Although he has often been interpreted as subscribing to a dictational view of Scripture, Calvin can also be cited as one who did not press for mechanical precision of every scriptural detail. In his commentaries, for example, he observes that the Gospel writers were unconcerned with such details as how many angels or women were present at Christ's empty tomb, or with numerical minutiae in the Old Testament. Calvin affirmed a subjective, Spirit-inspired validation of the Bible as the Word of God.

Like Calvin, Martin Luther (1483–1546) declared the full authority of Scripture, but did not propose or defend a particular view of inspiration. Consequently, both liberals and conservatives often quote him in support of their particular views. Harold Lindsell, for example, cites Luther in support of inerrancy while William Hordern, author of *A Layman's Guide to Protestant Theology*, asserts that Luther expressed radical doubts about the canonicity of certain books and the infallibility of Scripture:

> For Luther the Bible was not literally true from cover to cover nor were all parts of equal value. He found that there was in the Bible itself a criterion by which the whole could be judged. That criterion was the message of salvation by grace through faith which is spoken through Christ to the heart of the believer. In light of this criterion he started a movement that resulted in dropping from the Protestant Bible the so-called Apocryphal books which are still in the Catholic Bible. He questioned whether the books of Esther and Revelation should be in the Bible. He did not place much value on James' Epistle. He recognized that some of the forecasts of the prophets were in error, so that the Bible is by no means infallibly correct in all details.[3]

Sola Scriptura, as the reformers used the phrase, referred to the Bible as the supreme source of revelation. "Scripture is its own interpreter" was another basic Reformation maxim. It was the Reformers, too, who first coined the phrase, "the Bible is the infallible rule of faith and practice," meaning that Scripture, when rightly understood, accomplishes its purpose of bringing individuals into the full knowledge of the redeeming love of God in Christ. Lewis stands firmly in the Reformation tradition.

WHAT HAPPENED AFTER THE REFORMATION?

As time passed, the Protestant movement apparently felt the need to acknowledge an absolute, infallible authority equal to that of the Pope. By the seventeenth century, Scripture had become what has been called "the paper-Pope of Protestantism." Every word of Scripture, it was claimed, was *dictated* directly by God. Even the punctuation in the Bible was often said to be inspired. Before the end of the seventeenth century, we have the famous Puritan leader, John Owen (1616–83), dogmatically asserting:

> God was so with them [the Bible writers], and by the Holy Spirit so spake in them—as to their receiving of the Word from Him, and their delivering it unto others by speaking or writing —as that they were not themselves enabled, any habitual light, knowledge or conviction of truth, to declare His mind and will, but only acted as they were immediately moved by Him. Their tongue in what they said, or their hand in what they wrote, was no more at their own disposal than the pen is in the hand of an expert writer.[4]

Paul S. Rees, editor-at-large for *World Vision* magazine, in his article "Are We Trying to Outdo the Reformers?" in which Owen is quoted, remarks: "John Owen, in the above pronouncement, has been trapped into an effort to do what the Reformers wisely refrained from attempting; namely, trying to define precisely the mode, the mechanics, the techniques, by means of which the Bible became the vehicle of the revelation God intended."[5]

The fundamental purpose of Scripture, Lewis reminds us, "is to convey God's Word to the reader, [who] also needs His inspiration." Though Scripture is divinely inspired, its humanness is also apparent. As Lewis recognizes, "Naïvety, error, contradiction, even (as in the cursing Psalms) wickedness are not removed. The total result is not 'the Word of God' in the sense that every passage, in itself, gives impeccable science or history. It carries the Word of God. . . ."[6]

WITH THE AGE OF REASON CAME THE LIBERAL POSITION

The Enlightenment of the eighteenth century cast doubt on the historical reliability of Scripture. The Bible, which for centuries had been treated solely as a divine book, began to be treated as a mere human book. Rationalism raised its voice against traditionalism. Theologians, themselves committed to rationalistic presuppositions, were forced to compromise their view of inspiration. The Bible could no longer be taken at face value. Protagoras's famous dictum became gospel: "Man is the measure of all things."

In the nineteenth century religious liberalism arose. It was a bold attempt to synthesize the rationalism of the Enlightenment with the sacred sentiments of essential Christianity. Friedrich Schleiermacher, the father of modern liberal theology, had introduced subjectivism into Christian thought. He regarded the Bible as nothing more than a classical expression of religious experience, a record of man's search for Ultimate Reality.

Biblical inspiration, in the liberal view, is human insight by men of faith who sought to understand and communicate to others the mysteries of God. Scripture, therefore, is not inerrant, for the authors were limited by the outlook and interpretation of their times.

Liberal scholarship is guilty of committing what Lewis calls "chronological snobbery," that is, "the uncritical acceptance of the intellectual climate common to our own age and the assumption that whatever has gone out of date is on that account discredited." If the miraculous, for example, is no longer an "acceptable" idea in the modern world, one should ask "why it went out of date. Was it ever refuted (and if so by whom, where, and how conclusively) or did it merely die away as fashions do?" [7]

NEOORTHODOXY: RETURN TO ORTHODOXY OR RELIGIOUS COP-OUT?

From the womb of nineteenth-century liberalism, neoorthodoxy was born. Equally dissatisfied with the modern assumptions of liberalism and the supposed naïve assumptions of the older orthodoxy, neoorthodox theologians adopted many liberal presuppositions along with an existential commitment to special revelation and the traditional doctrines of orthodoxy.

Two names primarily are identified with neoorthodoxy: Karl Barth (1886–1968) and Emil Brunner (1889–1966). A third personality, Søren Kierkegaard (1813–55), is regarded as a forerunner. Their impact on modern theology is paramount, particularly concerning the nature of biblical inspiration.

Although neoorthodoxy was founded by Karl Barth, it was Emil Brunner who introduced Barth's ideas to America. According to Brunner, God does not reveal information (doctrines) about himself, he reveals himself. The Bible is not to be identified as the Word of God, which comes to man through subjective, experiential encounter. The Bible, rather, becomes the Word of God as God reveals himself through it.

"Truth as encounter" is Brunner's phrase to describe the subjective quality of the Word of God revealed to man through a personal encounter with Jesus Christ, the Living Word. The Bible serves as a *witness* to that Word, and is not revelation itself. In this view, Scripture is not inerrant, yet it has the authority of authors who know by experience the truth about which they write. Their "witness" may evoke a similar experience in the reader.

The Danish existentialist philosopher, Søren Kierkegaard, inspired many neoorthodox tendencies. He had said that when man reflects on his predicament and faces the harsh reality of a seemingly absurd universe, he is driven to despair. At that existential moment he is ready to grasp the salvation God offers him in Jesus Christ. Christianity is not a philosophy about God but a redemptive act of the Father. One becomes a Christian by a "leap of faith"—daring to believe that God has revealed himself in a moment of encounter.

Nothing in life is completely certain, of course, but Christianity is a reasonable risk. It fits the facts as we see them better than any other ideology. Faith requires a leap in the dark and a gamble that there really is a God, that he is not silent, and that he cares. The essence of faith is betting one's life on an existential encounter with God in Christ which alone gives life meaning.

Neoorthodox existentialism, while attractive in many ways

and containing much truth and insight, is basically a cop-out regarding the issue of biblical inspiration. In acknowledging only a subjective basis to revelation and religious meaning, neoorthodoxy gives license to believe most anything that is convenient and covers a multitude of sins.

Lewis comes close to a neoorthodox position when he says the Bible "carries" the Word of God. But by the verb *carry,* he does not mean what neoorthodox theologians mean when they say the Bible "becomes" or "contains" God's Word. While appreciating the distinction between the *Word of God* and the *words of Scripture,* Lewis differs with neoorthodoxy in recognizing that there are real spiritual truths being conveyed through the words of Scripture. The Bible is not simply a witness to God's Word but is, in a literary package, the special revelation of God.

At the same time, Lewis would acknowledge that it is the ongoing revelation of God in Christ, not its embodiment in Scripture, which is infallible. It is the *message* of the living Word of God, not the *medium* of its expression, which is authoritative. Scripture, as the primary medium of divine revelation, conveys, presents, or as Lewis prefers, "carries" God's truth in finite human form.

EVANGELICALISM: A HOUSE DIVIDED

An evangelical, in many people's minds, is a "born-again" Christian who holds to the traditional tenets of Christian faith, is actively involved in personal evangelism, and accepts the full authority of Scripture.

Biblical inspiration is becoming a "watershed issue" in the evangelical world. Although there have been internal family feuds over the meaning of inspiration and the question of inerrancy, evangelicals have generally remained united in opposition to liberal and neoorthodox views of revelation and the Bible.

Evangelicals, for the most part, maintain that God not only reveals himself but also reveals information about himself that can be stated in ways that can be understood. The Bible as the written Word of God carries inspired truth about God and man.

The evangelical position can be distinguished from liberal theological approaches in at least two basic ways. First, evangelicals approach the Bible with a radically different world view than the liberals. They claim that the Bible cannot be approached like other ancient books. Scripture claims for itself a supernatural origin requiring a special method to be understood. Liberals, on the other hand, generally presuppose a world view in which the miraculous is improbable, if not impossible. Accordingly, the liberal critic searches for naturalistic causes of the miraculous so-called. Thus, the historicity of biblical miracles is dismissed and apparent prophecies are said to have been made after the fact.

The liberal "quest for the historical Jesus," celebrated by Albert Schweitzer in his book by that title, sought to get behind the miraculous and mythical layers of Scripture to ascertain what the "real" Jesus was like. Schweitzer was forced to view the Jesus of history as a mild-mannered ethical preacher-type, who proclaimed an imminent apocalypse and died in attempt to bring it about.

The evangelical looks at the historic Jesus, miracles and all, and accepts him at face value. The liberal critic (from the evangelical perspective) lets his imagination go wild and works out ingenious theories to explain what really occurred. Presupposing that miracles are impossible and that Jesus was mistaken, the liberal attitude is neither critical nor scientific but based on dogmatic faith.

A second basic distinction between evangelicals and liberals is their understanding of divine disclosure. As discussed in chapter 1, revelation can be viewed as either personal encounter or propositional communication. Evangelicals, in affirming the latter, posit an infallible Scripture as the written Word of God. Liberals, in affirming truth as encounter, dichotomize the Word of God and the words of Scripture. If God's revelation is infallible while its representation in Scripture is fallible, evangelicals argue, then the infallible Word is of no consequence to man if it must be approached through a fallible record. If God inspired men of faith to receive revelation, then there is no reason why he should withhold inspiration from man's communication of that revelation.

Lewis would side with the evangelicals on these two distinctive points—world view and revelation—but would qualify the word *inspiration*. In the evangelical tradition, there are those who subscribe to a verbal view of inspiration in which inerrancy extends to the individual words of Scripture. There are other evangelicals who favor a plenary view of inspiration in which the Bible, *taken as a whole*, is affirmed as an infallible authority. What the Bible teaches regarding faith and practice is inerrant.

Lewis, though he never used the term, holds a literary view of inspiration. The Bible is inspired literature carrying a divine message. Human in its origin, biblical literature has been "raised by God above itself, qualified by Him to serve purposes which of itself it would not have served." [8]

Christians who maintain that the Bible is free from error in all matters (including science, history, biography and factual detail) are often classified as fundamentalists. [9] A few fundamentalists go to the extreme position of saying that God dictated his truth, word for word, to human recorders. Most fundamentalists, however, assert that the Bible in its original autographs was verbally inspired. The Holy Spirit of God, they believe, providentially prepared the author's personalities and writing styles and supernaturally superintended the writing process so that no errors or distortions of God's truth crept in. What is in the Bible is exactly what God wanted written. Since God is the author of Holy Scriptures and since he cannot lie, it is only logical to conclude, as do Harold Lindsell and Francis Schaeffer, that the Bible is without error in its entire scope.

"The issue," asserts Schaeffer, "is whether the Bible is God's verbalized communication to men giving propositionally *true* truth where it touches the cosmos and history or whether it is only in some sense 'revelational' where it touches matters of religion." [10]

Lindsell likewise endorses a fundamentalist view of inspiration: "However limited may have been their knowledge, and however much they may have erred when they were not writing sacred Scripture, the authors of Scripture, under the guidance of the Holy Spirit, were preserved from making factual, historical, scientific, or other errors." [11]

Fundamentalists believe that unless the Bible is verbally inspired and totally inerrant, it cannot be authoritative. The whole of Scripture stands or falls on the accuracy of its parts. If one part is in error, the whole Bible is suspect. As Lindsell emphatically states, "God the Holy Spirit by nature cannot lie or be the author of untruth. If the Scripture is inspired at all it must be infallible. If any part of it is not infallible, then that part cannot be inspired. If inspiration allows for the possibility of error then inspiration ceases to be inspiration." [12]

Lewis, as we have seen in the scope of this study, stands in sharp contrast to evangelical fundamentalism. His example proves that one can be a dedicated evangelical, accept the full authority of Scripture, yet disbelieve in inerrancy.

Lewis's view of literary inspiration recognizes revelation as God's disclosure of himself and his truth to inspired human beings, yet qualifies the precision with which divine truth can be transposed and communicated.

At the same time, Lewis insists that the issue of inspiration is far less important than evangelicals often make it out to be. Our real task, Lewis would say, is not to focus on life's "pointers" and "signposts" to God and his kingdom, but to get on with the journey at hand:

> When we are lost in the woods the sight of a signpost is a great matter. He who first sees it cries, "Look!" The whole party gathers round and stares. But when we have found the road and are passing signposts every few miles, we shall not stop and stare. They will encourage us and we shall be grateful to the authority that they set up. But we shall not stop and stare, or not much; not on this road, though their pillars are of silver and their lettering of gold. "We would be at Jerusalem." [13]

–6–

A Treasure in Earthen Vessels

No net less wide than a man's whole heart, nor less fine
a mesh than love, will hold the sacred Fish.
                              —*Reflections on the Psalms* [1]

In these chapters I have tried to determine what one great
Christian thinker thought about Scripture. C. S. Lewis's
thoughts are best summarized in his short phrase in *Reflections
on the Psalms*, that we should understand Scripture not as "the
conversion of God's word into a literature," but as the "taking
up of a literature to be a vehicle of God's word." [2]

Biblical inspiration is a mystery no less than the Incarnation.
Any attempt to appreciate the method and extent of divine
revelation and inspiration must first reverence the truth expressed in Isaiah 55:8–9: "For my thoughts are not your
thoughts, neither are your ways my ways, says the Lord. For as
the heavens are higher than the earth, so are my ways higher
than your ways and my thoughts than your thoughts."

As unsystematic as he is, Lewis holds by faith a high view of
Scripture. Not only were the biblical writers divinely inspired,
he believes, but those who preserved and canonized the sacred
writings as well as the editors, copyists, and translators who
modified them were supernaturally guided by God. The end
product, the Holy Bible as we have it today, can be accepted as

fully inspired, reliable and authoritative. The question of inerrancy dissolves, for Lewis, in light of his "literary" view of
inspiration.

How Should the Bible Be Read?

The Bible is fundamentally a sacred book, and "demands in-
cessantly to be taken on its own terms," says Lewis. "Stripped
. . . of its divine authority, stripped of its allegorical senses,
denied a romantic welcome," it cannot achieve its function.[3]

If the function of Scripture is to convey God's Word, we must
look beyond the language of the Bible (just as we must look
beyond imaginative literature or myth) to the reality it embodies.
We must learn to hear the message of Scripture by reading the
pages of the medium.

Lewis would admonish us to receive the message of Scripture
in the same way that we catch "the sacred Fish." The net required is "love"—an affirmative attitude toward the Word of
God in Scripture. The mesh needed is "a man's whole heart"—a
baptized literary embrace of the biblical images which allows us
to taste reality and be transformed.

An affirmative literary embrace of the message of Scripture
would not negate, in Lewis's opinion, Paul's teaching on the
submission of a wife to her husband, for example. An honest
reading of Scripture would attempt to get behind Paul's culturally conditioned language to the divine principle of submission being conveyed. To reject Paul's hierarchical view in
principle as culturally relative and accept egalitarian feminism
is not to embrace with loving affirmation the intended message
of the Bible. It is one thing to look beyond the words of Scripture to its embodied message, yet quite another to dismiss its
intended meaning.[4]

An affirmative literary embrace of the message of Scripture
would affirm the physical reality of heaven and hell, though not
perhaps their literal descriptions. The reality of angels, demons,
miracles and prophecy likewise is clearly a part of the intended
message of Scripture. The medium of expression may be cul-
tural, but the message is not.

The Bible as a *medium* should be approached in the same way as other literature (poetry should be read as poetry, drama as drama, history as history, legend as legend), yet its *message* is to be received as inspired and authoritative. The Bible as literature may contain error, but received by faith as a vehicle of God's Word, it teaches none.

To fully grasp the essential message of the Bible, an intuitive approach to its literary images is necessary. To try to abstract truth rationally from Scripture or to reduce embodied Reality to absolute propositions is "like trying to bottle a sunbeam." [5] The Bible simply is not meant to be read that way.

THE PROBLEM OF AUTHORITY: WE ARE NOT CONTENT

Many Christians are not content with the way Scripture seems to present itself. We prefer an infallible authority, divine in nature, absolute in certainty, universal in scope, and eternal in duration which will serve as a final measure or reference point of truth. To insist on such authority in Scripture, however, is to deny its humanness. It comes close to substituting a text as the object of one's faith for the One whom the text is about. If God chose to express himself through the frailty of human words, just as he chose to reveal himself through the frailty of human form, are we to question his wisdom? The living God spoke our language and shared our flesh, and there are limitations to both.

Christians sometimes find it difficult to accept such limitations. We insist on the whole truth delivered to us systematically in absolute propositions, nicely bound in an infallible book. To demand this of Scripture is to fail to recognize that God's infinite wisdom exceeds man's ability to conceptualize it. Though the Bible brings us inspired revelation from God, it comes to us through finite men who could not comprehend it in its fullness. Just as light is refracted by the glass through which it passes, so "we see through a glass darkly" and only "know in part." Divine revelation is sometimes distorted or at best abstracted by the personalities through which it comes. Though we do have conceptual truth in Scripture, it is only approximate. The divine light is obscured by the medium through which it shines.

What we have in the Bible (literary truth) may not be what we would have preferred (absolute, propositional truth)—"something we could have tabulated and memorized and relied on like the multiplication table," as Lewis says. The fact is that Scripture does not present us with "unrefracted light giving us ultimate truth in systematic form." Instead we have an inspired embodiment of divine revelation, through which God continues to reveal himself to us today. To fully appreciate the Bible, we should not use it as an encyclopedia of systematic truth, but rather live in it by "steeping ourselves in its tone or temper and so learning its over-all message." [6]

Sometimes we are tempted to think that God should have penned the Bible himself and presented it to us fresh from the eternal inkwell on a take-it-or-leave-it basis without any human element affecting its composition or obscuring its divine light. Life would have been so much simpler, we imagine, and Lewis seems to agree: "One can respect, and at moments envy, both the Fundamentalist's view of the Bible and the Roman Catholic's view of the Church." But there is nothing to be gained by wishful thinking. Our faith in the Bible and our attitude toward the way it is presented should be the humble recognition, as Lewis consents, that "since this is what God has done, this . . . was best." [7]

Lewis also reminds us that the way the Bible presents itself is the same way that Christ presented himself so long ago:

> We may observe that the teaching of Our Lord Himself, in which there is no imperfection, is not given us in that cut-and-dried, fool-proof, systematic fashion we might have expected or desired. He wrote no book. We have only reported sayings, most of them uttered in answer to questions, shaped in some degree by their context. And when we have collected them all we cannot reduce them to a system. [8]

In Christ were the words of eternal life, yet he spoke in parables, in paradoxes, in riddles. Divine truth is revealed, not to the cut-and-dried literalist, but to those whose spiritual eyes have been opened, whose literary palates have been sensitized, whose imaginations have been baptized. "There is almost no 'letter' in the words of Jesus. Taken by a literalist, He will always prove the most elusive of teachers. Systems cannot keep up with that darting illumination. No net less wide than a man's whole heart, nor less fine a mesh than love, will hold the sacred Fish." [9]

Conclusion: A Treasure Chest of Truth

The unique contribution of C. S. Lewis to the present controversy over inerrancy is in helping us view the Bible as human literature carrying a divine message.

This divine message, Lewis would have us remember, is not confined to the medium of Scripture. God, the Source of all truth, in the process of "reconciling the world unto himself," has used many means to call his sheep back into the fold: He has inspired great myths and literature throughout history, created in us immortal longings, spoken to us through conscience and religious experience, and given us Holy Scripture to convey his message. And finally, he has revealed himself in human form, died, and risen again so that we might die and live with him.

Because of God's initiative in revelation, we possess a treasure chest of truth that is of eternal value. God's Word is the "treasure" revealed through "earthen vessels," as 2 Corinthians 4:7 implies: "But we have this treasure in earthen vessels to show that the transcendent power belongs to God and not to us." Let us not mistake the vessels for the treasure nor fail to find the treasure in the vessels.

Appendix A
Two Letters from C. S. Lewis

Dear Mr. Carnell, I am myself a little uneasy about the question you raise: there seems to be almost equal objection to the position taken up in my footnote * and to its alternative of attributing the same kind and degree of historicity to all the books of the Bible. You see, the question about Jonah and the great fish does not turn simply on intrinsic probability. The point is that the whole *Book of Jonah* has to me the air of being a moral romance, a quite different kind of thing from, say the account of King David or the New

---

* This refers to the footnote on p. 139 of the Macmillan paperback edition of *Miracles* (p. 161 of the English edition) in which Lewis suggests that God's truth, "on the documentary side . . . first appears in *mythical* form and then by a long process of condensing or focussing finally becomes incarnate as History. . . . Whether we can ever say with certainty where in this process of crystalization any particular Old Testament story falls, is another matter. I take it that the memoirs of David's court come at one end of the scale and are scarcely less historical than *St. Mark* or *Acts*; and that the *Book of Jonah* is at the opposite end."

[97]

Testament narratives, not pegged, like them, into any historical situation.

In what sense does the Bible "present" the Jonah story "as historical"? Of course, it doesn't say "This is fiction," but then neither does our Lord say that the Unjust Judge, Good Samaritan, or Prodigal Son are fiction. (I would put *Esther* in the same category as *Jonah* for the same reason.) How does a denial, a doubt, of their historicity lead logically to a similar denial of New Testament miracles. Supposing (as I think is the case), that sound critical reading revealed different *kinds* of narrative in the Bible, surely it would be illogical to suppose that these different kinds should all be read in the same way?

This is not a "rationalistic approach" to miracles. Where I doubt the historicity of an Old Testament narrative I never do so on the ground that the miraculous as such is incredible. Nor does it deny a unique sort of inspiration: allegory, parable, romance, and lyric might be inspired as well as chronicle. I wish I could direct you to a good book on the subject, but I don't know one. With all good wishes, yours sincerely, C. S. Lewis.

PAGE OF NOTES WITH LETTER FROM C. S. LEWIS
TO CLYDE S. KILBY, MAY 7, 1959

Whatever view we hold of the divine authority of Scripture must make room for the following facts.
1. The distinction which St. Paul makes in 1 Cor vii between οὐκ ἐγὼ ἀλλ᾽ ὁ κύριος (v. 10) and ἐγὼ λέγω, οὐχ ὁ κυριος (v. 12).
2. The apparent inconsistencies between the genealogies in Matt i and Luke iii; with the accounts of the death of Judas in Matt. xxvii 5 and Acts i. 18–19.
3. St. Luke's own account of how he obtained his matter (i. 1–4).
4. The universally admitted unhistoricity (I do not say, of course, falsity) of at least some narratives in Scripture (the parables), which may well extend also to Jonah and Job.
5. If every good and perfect gift comes from the Father of lights then all true and edifying writings, whether in Scripture or not, must be *in some sense* inspired.
6. John xi. 49–52 Inspiration may operate in a wicked man without his knowing it, and he can then utter the untruth he intends

(propriety of making an innocent man a political scapegoat) *as well as* the truth he does not intend (the divine sacrifice).

It seems to me that 2 and 4 rule out the view that every statement in Scripture must be *historical* truth. And 1, 3, 5, and 6 rule out the view that inspiration is a single thing in the sense that, if present at all, it is always present in the same mode and the same degree. Therefore, I think, rule out the view that any one passage taken in isolation can be assumed to be inerrant in exactly the same sense as any other: e.g. that the numbers of O.T. armies (which in view of the size of the country, if true, involve continuous miracle) are statistically correct because the story of the Resurrection is historically correct. That the over-all operation of Scripture is to convey God's Word to the reader (he also needs his inspiration) who reads it in the right spirit, I fully believe. That it *also* gives true answers to all the questions (often religiously irrelevant) which he might ask, I don't. The very *kind* of truth we are often demanding was, in my opinion, not even envisaged by the ancients.

Appendix B
Lewis: The Rational Romantic

As a rationalist, Lewis approached the message of the Bible as a truth to be believed. As a romantic, he approached the message of the Bible as a reality to be received. Lewis's literary view of inspiration encompassed both his rational faculty for understanding and his romantic intuition to find meaning.

"I am a rationalist," states Lewis in his essay "Bluspels and Flalansferes." "For me, reason is the natural organ of truth; but imagination is the organ of meaning." [1] What does he mean by this statement? What is the relationship between truth and meaning, reason and imagination, and which is primary?

Reason and imagination for Lewis are the complementary human faculties for knowing. In the realm of facts, empirical evidence, sense objects, particulars, and so on, truth is known through reason. But transcendent Reality—knowledge of universals in the eternal realm—if it is to be known at all, must be grasped by imagination. In this respect Lewis was a romantic and his imagination primary.

While reason perceives the truth or falsity of particulars, imagination apprehends universals (though never in an absolute way). What is conveyed through imagination, Lewis says, "is not truth but reality," carefully distinguishing between the two: "Truth is always *about* something, but reality is that *about which* truth is." [2]

Reality, then, is concrete and absolute, while truth is abstract and approximate. Statements, philosophies, and theories about reality, though they may be true in a partial, abstract sense, are not reality itself. No theory of art, for example, can tell us what art means. So with reality, whose organ of meaning is imagination.

The imaginative approach to reality is the nineteenth-century romantic affirmation of intuition over discursive reason, feeling over intellect, and the heart over the head, as the primary faculty of knowing. Imagination serves to grasp the essence of reality, intuit the immaterial universals, and embrace meaningful images—images which then become the tools of reason. But without the prior work of the imagination, reasoning itself is impossible.

In describing his friend Charles Williams as a "Christian Romantic," Lewis offers the following definition:

> A romantic theologian does not mean one who is romantic about theology, but one who is theological about romance, one who considers the theological implications of those experiences which are called romantic. The belief that the most serious and ecstatic experiences either of human love or of imaginative literature have such theological implications, and that they can be healthy and fruitful only if the implications are diligently thought out and severely lived, is the root principle of all his work.[3]

"Christian Romanticism" is a fairly descriptive term not only for the religious views of Charles Williams but for other Oxford Christians as well, including J. R. R. Tolkien, Owen Barfield, and C. S. Lewis.

Williams, for one, had a profound influence on Lewis's romantic spirit. From him he learned that theology could not be completely domesticated by reason. The mysteries of faith could not be reduced to a precise, logical system, nor the tensions, paradoxes, and contradictions inherent in Christianity reconciled. The origin of evil or the problem of suffering, for example, have never been adequately resolved. Lewis recalls how he was profoundly humbled on one occasion when Williams compared Job's "comforters" to "the sort of people who write books on the Problem of Pain."[4]

Williams's influence is also apparent in Lewis's emphasis on *Sehnsucht*—the romantic quest for the imagined ideal. An analysis of *Sehnsucht*, being central to romantic theology and indicative of Lewis's rational-romantic faith, will occupy the remainder of this appendix.

The experience of *Sehnsucht* is one of intense desire and longing, and it is worth quoting again Lewis's description of it from *Mere Christianity*:

> Most people, if they had really learned to look into their own hearts, would know that they do want and want acutely, something that cannot be had in this world. There are all sorts of things in this world that offer to give it to you, but they never quite keep their promise. The longing which arises in us when we first fall in love, or first think of some foreign country, or first take up some subject that excites us, are longings which no marriage, no travel, no learning, can really satisfy.[5]

Whatever form the romantic ideal assumes (a perfect beloved, an ideal vacation, a distant hill), the desire always proves elusive. We are continually separated from what we so earnestly long for. Nothing satisfies the sweet desire of the soul, as Lewis acutely recognizes:

> Lust can be gratified. Another personality can become to us 'our America, our New-found-land!' A happy marriage can be achieved. But what has any of these three, or any mixture of the three, to do with that unnameable something, desire for which pierces us like a rapier at the smell of a bonfire, the sound of wild ducks flying overhead, the title of *The Well at the World's End*, the opening lines of *Kubla Khan*, the morning cobwebs in late summer, or the noise of falling waves?[6]

Sehnsucht may be triggered, as Chad Walsh expresses, "by a bar of music, a landscape, a forgotten memory." "The experience is an instantaneous sense of seeing into the heart of things, as though a universe beyond the universe opened itself wide for an instant and as instantly slammed its doors shut. It is an experience the Romantic poets, such as Wordsworth, often describe, and it has parallels with some kinds of religious mysticism."[7]

Two things can be said about the experience of *Sehnsucht*:

First, though our sense of desire is intense, and at times even painful, the *wanting* itself is a delight. No other experience life can offer compares to the joy of romantic longing. Even when there is no hope for the fulfillment of the desire, the quest itself is meaningful for its own sake. We relentlessly try to catch a falling star "no matter how hopeless, no matter how far"; we are intent on chasing an illusive dream "that shines so fair, but when found isn't there." The romantic quest for the ideal is not something to be lightly relinquished but profoundly cherished. "Our *wantings* are our best *havings*," Lewis wrote in a letter, paraphrasing George MacDonald.

Second, the *object* of the desire remains a mystery. We don't know exactly what we want. When what we think we want is at last satisfied, we find the same desire for a new object. Even when we think seriously of what it would be like to actually attain our imagined ideal, the magic is lost for us and the desire suddenly shifts ground. "Once grant your fairy, your enchanted forest, your satyr, faun, wood-nymph and well of immortality *real*," stated Lewis, "and amidst all the scientific, social, and practical interest which the discovery would awake, the Sweet Desire would have disappeared, would have shifted its ground, like the cuckoo's voice or the rainbow's end, and be now calling us from beyond a *further* hill." [8]

Given the universal experience of *Sehnsucht*, Lewis identifies two wrong and one right way to deal with the persistent fact.

The "Fool's Way" is one of *projection* of blame on the objects of desire themselves. The Fool goes through life thinking that if only he had another woman or more money, or a better vacation, or a more expensive home or car or whatever, then happiness would truly be his. Such people, Lewis observes, are usually bored, disappointed, and forever unhappy.

"The Way of the Disillusioned 'Sensible Man'" is one of *passive acceptance* of the way things are. Having given up youthful chasing of the rainbow's end, he settles down and learns not to expect too much out of life. After all, we were never promised a rose garden. Along with the sunshine there's got to be a little rain sometime. He represses that part of his soul which once cried to the moon or chased falling stars. This view would be the best of all possible views, Lewis admits, if man were not immortal.

The Romantic or "the Christian Way" is one of *affirmation*. The Christian believes "creatures are not born with desires unless satisfaction for those desires exists." Basic human longings, by nature, imply potential fulfillment. Lewis's ontological proof for the immortality of the soul simply reads as follows:

A baby feels hunger: well, there is such a thing as food. A duckling wants to swim: well, there is such a thing as water. Men feel sexual desire: well, there is such a thing as sex. If I find in myself a desire which no experience in this world can satisfy, the most probable explanation is that I was made for another world. If none of my earthly pleasures satisfy it, that does not prove that the universe is a fraud. Probably earthly pleasures were never meant to satisfy it, but only to arouse it, to suggest the real thing.[9]

As was stated in chapter 4, the fact that the best of life's pleasures are only half-pleasures compared to our imagined ideal is God's way of giving us a taste of what heaven is like, a thirst for our true home. Corbin Scott Carnell personifies *Sehnsucht* as the "hound of Heaven, relentlessly pursuing man in order that he may discover his true identity and home." [10] The final fulfillment of *Sehnsucht* is portrayed beautifully in *The Last Battle* where the Narnian unicorn shouts with joy:

> "I have come home at last! This is my real country! I belong here. This is the land I have been looking for all my life, though I never knew it till now. The reason why we loved the old Narnia is that it sometimes looked a little like this." [11]

Lewis confidently believes "that if a man diligently followed" the romantic road of Desire, "pursuing the false objects until their falsity appeared and then resolutely abandoning them," he would finally discover the eternal source of his longing.[12] Lewis himself is one individual who proved all the supposed fulfillments of *Sehnsucht* wrong. He makes the claim rather modestly in his preface to the paperback edition of *The Pilgrim's Regress*:

> I know them to be wrong not by intelligence but by experience, such experience as would not have come my way if my youth had been wiser, more virtuous, and less self-centred than it was. For I have myself been deluded by every one of these false answers in turn, and have contemplated each of them earnestly enough to discover the cheat.[13]

Lewis's spiritual pilgrimage of trying to "fill his cup with false hopes," finally finding the well of Living Water, is sensitively portrayed in two books, *Surprised by Joy* and *The Pilgrim's Regress*. The *Sehnsucht* motif, however, can be identified in nearly all his works.

Surprised by Joy is Lewis's spiritual autobiography in which he discloses, he says, "the shape of my early life." Born in Ireland in 1898, the son of cultured parents, Lewis claims to have had a relatively happy childhood. His first experience of *Sehnsucht* came from looking out his nursery windows when he was six and seeing the "Green Hills" in the distance. Similar emotions were aroused in him as he read extensively, drew pictures, wrote animal stories, and lived almost entirely in his imagination.

At ten, Lewis was sent off to school in England for a period of two years—a rather grim experience, he recalls. After a brief year back home, he returned to England to Cherbourg House, a preparatory school for Malvern College. There he suffered spiritually from the conflict between his avowed atheism and his anger at God for not existing. His desire for Joy intensified as he began reading Norse mythology and assimilating the beauty of nature. At Malvern College he became absorbed in the world of books, and at sixteen was ready to begin preparation for university under a private tutor.

W. T. Kirkpatrick—an atheistic, logical positivist-type Scotsman —ruthlessly drilled Lewis for two years on his dialectic, pursuing every word the boy spoke, citing inconsistencies in speech, hasty generalizations, and other logical fallacies. Kirkpatrick's rationalism taught Lewis respect for reason and strengthened his atheism, but his romantic spirit survived and flourished. He preferred reading fantasies and romances, responding imaginatively to their suggestions of romantic longing.

A turning point came when Lewis read George MacDonald's *Phantastes,* which had a profound impact on his imagination. "It was as though the voice which had called to me from the world's end was now speaking at my side," he writes. Through reading MacDonald, his imagination was "baptized," furthering him along the path to God with renewed romantic vision.

At nineteen, he won a classical scholarship to Oxford and there met Owen Barfield—"the wisest and best of my unofficial teachers." He met J. R. R. Tolkien there as well, along with many other Christians who served to break down his prejudices against Christianity.

Following army service and graduation, Lewis lectured for a year in Philosophy and was elected the following year, at twenty-six, a fellow of Magdalen College. His philosophical presuppositions were severely challenged as a tutor; his search for Joy intensified. It appeared to him that the Hound of Heaven was demanding his soul's total surrender. Afraid and under deep conviction, he wished only to be left alone:

> You must picture me alone in that room in Magdalen, night after night, feeling, whenever my mind lifted even for a second from my work, the steady, unrelenting approach of Him whom I so earnestly

desired not to meet. That which I greatly feared had at last come upon me. In the Trinity Term of 1929 I gave in, and admitted that God was God, and knelt and prayed: perhaps, that night, the most dejected and reluctant convert in all England.[14]

In *The Pilgrim's Regress,* which was intended, according to the subtitle, as an "Allegorical Apology for Christianity, Reason and Romanticism," Lewis attempted to portray his search for Joy. Although he admits in the Preface to the third edition that the word *Romanticism* has become so broad that it has lost its meaning, he makes it clear that *Sehnsucht* was essentially what he meant to convey by the term when he wrote the allegory in the 1930s.

The Pilgrim's Regress is the story of a pilgrim, John, born in Puritania, who learns at an early age that a mysterious Landlord owns everything, yet forbids him license to do much of anything. He is both guilt-ridden by imposed religious duties he fails to perform, and haunted by a strange desire which turns his whole life into a romantic quest. John hears sweet music coming from a source unseen and a voice saying "come." As he catches a glimpse of an island to the west surrounded by a calm sea, an overwhelming yearning seizes him. He becomes obsessed with finding the island of his dream.

On the quest, John encounters the allegorical equivalents of nearly every philosophical position and political ideology imaginable. Nothing seems to satisfy his deep desire. Finally, he accepts the reasonable advice of Mother Kirk (the Church, standing for Christianity), who tells him of the Source of his longing and the Answer to his heart's dream. Like Augustine, he was restless until he found his proper rest.

Lewis's intellectual journey, like that of his character John, had been "from 'popular realism' to philosophical Idealism; from Idealism to Pantheism; from Pantheism to Theism; and from Theism to Christianity"—to him a very natural progression.[15]

Lewis chose to embody in allegory the truth he gained from his romantic quest because he believed the highest spiritual realities could only be communicated symbolically and received imaginatively. Allegory, at its best, "approaches myth, which must be grasped with the imagination, not with the intellect." [16]

Such is Lewis's rational-romantic synthesis of truth and meaning, reason and imagination. Reason alone cannot lead us to truth. But neither can truth be understood apart from reason. Both reason and imagination, seemingly at odds with one another, are necessary for truth to be meaningful.

Reconciling reason and imagination is no easy task, as Lewis is the first to admit. *Till We Have Faces*, in part, is his attempt to reconcile them. His poem entitled, "Reason" is an appeal for a divine synthesis:

> Oh who will reconcile in me both maid and mother,
> Who make in me a concord of the depth and height?
> Who make imagination's dim exploring touch
> Ever report the same as intellectual sight?
> Then could I truly say, and not deceive,
> Then wholly say, that I BELIEVE.[17]

Notes

CHAPTER 1

1. Letter from C. S. Lewis to Clyde S. Kilby. The complete page of notes from which this quotation is taken is given in Appendix A. It also appears in *Letters of C. S. Lewis*, edited, with a memoir by W. H. Lewis, p. 287. Full information on works cited is given in the bibliography.

2. Francis A. Schaeffer, *No Final Conflict*, p. 48.

3. Fuller Theological Seminary, *Theology, News and Notes* (Pasadena: Fuller Theological Seminary, 1976), p. 4.

4. Harold Lindsell, *The Battle for the Bible*, p. 210.

5. Harold Lindsell, in an editorial "Are Evangelicals Outward Bound?" *Christianity Today*, March 26, 1976, p. 25.

6. C. S. Lewis, "God in the Dock," in *God in the Dock*, p. 181.

7. Richard B. Cunningham, *C. S. Lewis: Defender of the Faith*, jacket cover.

8. C. S. Lewis, *Reflections on the Psalms*, p. 27.

9. Ibid., p. 96.

10. For the complete quotation, see Appendix A.

11. C. S. Lewis, *The World's Last Night and Other Essays*, pp. 93–94.

12. C. S. Lewis, *Transposition and Other Addresses*, p. 19.

13. C. S. Lewis, "Rejoinder to Dr. Pittenger," *God in the Dock,* p. 183.

14. Ibid.

CHAPTER 2

1. Lewis, *Reflections on the Psalms,* p. 92.
2. Edgar W. Boss, "The Theology of C. S. Lewis" (Th.D. dissertation submitted to Northern Baptist Theological Seminary, Chicago, 1948), reviewed by Clyde S. Kilby, *The Christian World of C. S. Lewis,* pp. 191–92.
3. C. S. Lewis, *Mere Christianity* (1960), p. 76.
4. Ibid., p. 43.
5. Ibid., p. 65.
6. C. S. Lewis, *The Last Battle,* pp. 164–65, emphasis mine.
7. Lewis, *Mere Christianity,* pp. 176–77.
8. Ibid., pp. 86–87.
9. C. S. Lewis, *The Great Divorce,* p. 65.
10. C. S. Lewis, *The Problem of Pain,* p. 115.
11. Lewis, *The Great Divorce,* p. 66.
12. Lewis, *Pain,* p. 115.
13. Lewis, *Mere Christianity,* p. 108.
14. Lewis, *The Great Divorce,* p. 32.
15. Ibid., p. 69.
16. Lewis, *Pain,* p. 116.
17. C. S. Lewis, *Letters to Malcolm: Chiefly on Prayer,* p. 108.
18. Lewis, *Mere Christianity,* p. 172.
19. Lewis, *Malcolm,* p. 108.
20. Lewis, *The Great Divorce,* p. vi.
21. Lewis, *Malcolm,* p. 15.
22. Ibid., p. 108.
23. Lewis, *Mere Christianity,* p. 62.
24. Lewis, *Malcolm,* p. 9.
25. Ibid., p. 103.
26. Ibid., p. 104.
27. Lewis, *Pain,* p. 60.
28. Ibid., pp. 64–68.
29. Ibid., pp. 124–27.
30. Lewis, *Mere Christianity,* pp. 57–61, passim.
31. Ibid., p. 157.
32. Lewis, *Reflections on the Psalms,* p. 92. Lewis may be in error in attributing the doubt to Calvin, who said in a sermon that he believed the Book of Job to be historical. Luther did express, however, such doubts as Lewis describes.
33. Letter from C. S. Lewis to Clyde S. Kilby, May 7, 1959, quoted in Kilby, *The Christian World of C. S. Lewis,* p. 153.

34. Lewis, *Reflections on the Psalms,* p. 93.

35. Lewis, *Pain,* p. 68.

36. Kilby, *The Christian World of C. S. Lewis,* p. 160.

37. Ibid., p. 153, citing letter of May 7, 1959.

38. Lewis, *The World's Last Night,* pp. 97–99, passim.

39. Lewis, "Modern Theology and Biblical Criticism," *Christian Reflections,* pp. 154, 155.

40. Ibid., p. 158.

41. Ibid., pp. 159–61, passim.

42. Lewis, *Malcolm,* p. 104.

43. Cunningham, *C. S. Lewis: Defender of the Faith,* p. 63.

44. Lewis, "Modern Theology and Biblical Criticism," pp. 152–53.

45. Lewis, *Malcolm,* p. 119.

46. Lewis, "Modern Theology and Biblical Criticism," p. 153.

47. Lewis, *Reflections on the Psalms,* p. 92.

48. Cunningham, *C. S. Lewis: Defender of the Faith,* p. 101.

49. Paul L. Holmer, *C. S. Lewis: The Shape of His Faith and Thought,* p. 6.

50. Cunningham, *C. S. Lewis: Defender of the Faith,* p. 101.

51. Holmer, *C. S. Lewis: The Shape of His Faith and Thought,* pp. 100–101.

CHAPTER 3

1. C. S. Lewis, "Christianity and Literature," *Christian Reflections,* p. 7.

2. C. S. Lewis, *An Experiment in Criticism,* pp. 88, 89.

3. Ibid., pp. 100–101.

4. Ibid., p. 137.

5. Ibid., pp. 18, 19.

6. Ibid., p. 141.

7. Ibid., p. 13.

8. Ibid., p. 106.

9. Ibid., p. 114.

10. C. S. Lewis and E. M. W. Tillyard, *The Personal Heresy: A Controversy,* p. 11.

11. Ibid., p. 23.

12. Ibid., pp. 29, 30.

13. Lewis is *not* saying that literature functions solely to teach moral truth. He rejects the so-called "didactic heresy" and states that literature by its very nature and definition must have artistic quality and invite good reading: "Every episode, explanation, description, dialogue—ideally every sentence—must be pleasurable and interesting for its own sake." Lewis believes that "a true lover of literature should be in one way like an honest examiner, who is prepared to give the highest marks to the

telling, felicitous and well-documented exposition of views he dissents from or even abominates" (*An Experiment in Criticism*, pp. 84, 86).

14. Philip Sidney, "An Apology for Poetry," in *Criticism: The Major Statements*, edited by Charles Kaplan (New York: St. Martin's Press, 1975), p. 120.

15. Lewis, *The Personal Heresy*, p. 109.

16. Lewis, *The Great Divorce*, pp. 77–78, 79.

17. Lewis, *The Personal Heresy*, p. 52.

18. See Appendix B, "Lewis: The Rational Romantic," for a summary discussion of Lewis's Christian Romanticism.

19. Lewis, *An Experiment in Criticism*, p. 139.

20. C. S. Lewis, *The Four Loves*, pp. 174, 175.

21. Holmer, *C. S. Lewis: The Shape of His Faith and Thought*, p. 22.

22. Lewis, "Myth Became Fact," *God in the Dock*, p. 65.

23. Holmer, *C. S. Lewis*, p. 39.

24. Ibid., p. 30.

25. Ibid., p. 20.

26. Ibid., p. 48.

27. Plato, *The Republic*, translated by Desmond Lee, p. 432.

28. Lewis, *Poems*, p. 11.

29. C. S. Lewis, "The Language of Religion," *Christian Reflections*, p. 129.

30. Ibid., p. 133.

31. Ibid., pp. 135–37, 141, passim.

32. Owen Barfield, "Poetic Diction and Legal Fiction," in *The Importance of Language*, edited by Max Black, p. 51.

33. Lewis, "The Language of Religion," p. 140.

34. C. S. Lewis, *A Grief Observed*, pp. 74–75.

35. *Webster's Seventh New Collegiate Dictionary*.

36. C. S. Lewis, "Bluspels and Flalansferes: A Semantic Nightmare," in *Selected Literary Essays*, pp. 254, 263. The essay also appears in *The Importance of Language*, edited by Max Black.

37. Lewis, *Poems*, p. 129.

38. C. S. Lewis, *The Pilgrim's Regress*, 2d ed., p. 146.

39. Lewis, "Myth Became Fact," p. 66.

40. Ibid., p. 65.

41. Ibid., p. 66.

CHAPTER 4

1. Lewis, *The Pilgrim's Regress*, p. 171.

2. Lewis, *The Four Loves*, p. 174.

3. C. S. Lewis, *Miracles: A Preliminary Study*, pp. 75–76.

4. Lewis, *The Four Loves*, p. 175.
5. Lewis, "Myth Became Fact," p. 66.
6. C. S. Lewis, *Perelandra*, p. 144.
7. Lewis, *Experiment in Criticism*, p. 43.
8. Lewis, *Pain*, p. 64, n. 1.
9. Lewis, *Miracles*, p. 139, n. 1.
10. C. S. Lewis, *Allegory of Love*, p. 47.
11. Lewis, *Experiment in Criticism*, p. 40.
12. Ibid., p. 41.
13. Ibid., p. 56.
14. Lewis, "Myth Became Fact," p. 66.
15. Lewis, *Perelandra*, p. 149.
16. C. S. Lewis, ed., *George MacDonald: An Anthology*, pp. 16–17.
17. Lewis, "Myth Became Fact," p. 66.
18. C. S. Lewis, *The Voyage of the Dawn Treader*, p. 201.
19. Lewis, *The Last Battle*, p. 171.
20. Ibid., pp. 169–70.
21. Lewis, *Miracles*, Appendix A.
22. Lewis, *Transposition and Other Addresses*. The essay "Transposition" (somewhat augmented) also appears in *They Asked for a Paper*, pp. 166–82.
23. Lewis, *Pilgrim's Regress*, pp. 58–59.
24. Lewis, *Transposition*, p. 17.
25. Plato, *The Republic*, pp. 307–8.
26. Lewis, *Pain*, p. 4.
27. C. S. Lewis, *Till We Have Faces*, p. 249.
28. Lewis, *Perelandra*, pp. 18–19.
29. Lewis, *Pain*, p. 21.
30. Lewis, *Mere Christianity*, p. 19.
31. Lewis, *Pain*, pp. 21–22.
32. Lewis, *Mere Christianity*, pp. 119, 120.
33. Corbin Scott Carnell, *Bright Shadow of Reality*, p. 144.
34. Lewis, *Mere Christianity*, p. 54.
35. Lewis, *Pilgrim's Regress*, pp. 152–55.
36. Lewis, *Mere Christianity*, p. 54.
37. Lewis, *Psalms*, p. 85.
38. Plato, *The Republic*, pp. 107–8.
39. Lewis, *Psalms*, p. 88.
40. Ibid., p. 89.
41. Douglas Gilbert and Clyde S. Kilby, *C. S. Lewis: Images of His World*, pp. 20–21.
42. Ibid.
43. C. S. Lewis, "Is Theology Poetry?" in *They Asked for a Paper*, p. 158.

44. Lewis, *Miracles*, p. 120.
45. Ibid., p. 116.
46. Lewis, *Psalms*, pp. 89–90.
47. Lewis, *Miracles*, p. 139, n. 1.
48. Lewis, *Pain*, p. 23.
49. C. S. Lewis, *Surprised by Joy*, p. 235.
50. Lewis, *Miracles*, p. 120.
51. Lewis, "Myth Became Fact," pp. 66–67.
52. Lewis, *Pilgrim's Regress*, p. 171.
53. Lewis, *Miracles*, p. 80.
54. Lewis, *Malcolm*, p. 51.
55. Ibid., p. 21.
56. Ibid., p. 52.
57. Ibid.
58. C. S. Lewis, "Horrid Red Things," in *God in the Dock*, p. 71.

CHAPTER 5

1. See Appendix A, for text of letter of C. S. Lewis to Clyde S. Kilby.
2. Lewis, *The Four Loves*, p. 175.
3. William Hordern, *A Layman's Guide to Protestant Theology*, rev. ed., p. 58.
4. Quoted by Paul S. Rees in *Theology, News and Notes* (Pasadena: Fuller Theological Seminary, 1976), p. 14.
5. Ibid.
6. Lewis, *Psalms*, p. 94.
7. Lewis, *Surprised by Joy*, pp. 107–8.
8. Lewis, *Psalms*, p. 111.
9. "The terms fundamentalist or conservative are not easy to define. Usually these terms are applied to anyone who believes in the verbal inspiration of the Bible, that is, the belief that the words of the Bible are the direct and errorless words of God" (Hordern, *Layman's Guide*, p. 57).
10. Schaeffer, *No Final Conflict*, p. 8.
11. Lindsell, *Battle for the Bible*, pp. 30–31.
12. Ibid.
13. Lewis, *Surprised by Joy*, p. 238.

CHAPTER 6

1. Lewis, *Psalms*, p. 100.
2. Ibid., p. 97.
3. C. S. Lewis, *The Literary Impact of the Authorised Version*, p.

97. This essay also appears in *They Asked for a Paper*, pp. 26–50, and in *Selected Literary Essays*, pp. 126–45.

4. Lewis says he stands with St. Paul in his hierarchical view of nature: "I do not believe that God created an egalitarian world. I believe in authority of the parent over child, husband over wife, learned over simple, to have been as much a part of the original plan as the authority of man over beast" ("Membership," in *Transposition and Other Addresses*, p. 40).

5. Lewis, *Psalms*, p. 95.

6. Ibid., p. 94.

7. Ibid., p. 95.

8. Ibid.

9. Ibid., p. 100.

Appendix B

1. Lewis, "Bluspels and Flalansferes," p. 265.

2. Lewis, "Myth Became Fact," p. 66, emphasis mine.

3. C. S. Lewis, "Preface," in *Essays Presented to Charles Williams*, edited by C. S. Lewis, p. vi.

4. Ibid., p. xiii.

5. Lewis, *Mere Christianity*, p. 119.

6. Lewis, *Pilgrim's Regress*, pp. 9, 10.

7. Lewis, *A Grief Observed*, pp. 74, 75.

8. Lewis, *Pilgrim's Regress*, p. 9.

9. Lewis, *Mere Christianity*, pp. 119–20.

10. Carnell, *Bright Shadow of Reality*, p. 144.

11. Lewis, *The Last Battle*, p. 171.

12. Lewis, *Pilgrim's Regress*, p. 10.

13. Ibid., p. 8.

14. Lewis, *Surprised by Joy*, pp. 228, 229.

15. Lewis, *Pilgrim's Regress*, p. 5.

16. Ibid., p. 13.

17. Lewis, *Poems*, p. 81.

Selected Bibliography

PRIMARY SOURCES—BOOKS BY C. S. LEWIS

The Abolition of Man. New York: The Macmillan Co., 1946.
Allegory of Love: A Study in Medieval Tradition. 1936. London: Oxford University Press paperback, 1958.
Christian Reflections. Edited by Walter Hooper. Grand Rapids: Wm. B. Eerdmans, 1967.
(Ed.) *Essays Presented to Charles Williams.* 1947. Reprint ed. Grand Rapids: Wm. B. Eerdmans, 1966.
An Experiment in Criticism. Cambridge: University Press, 1961.
The Four Loves. New York: Harcourt, Brace & World, 1960.
(Ed.) *George MacDonald: An Anthology.* New York: The Macmillan Co., 1947.
God in the Dock. Edited by Walter Hooper. Grand Rapids: Wm. B. Eerdmans, 1970.
The Great Divorce. New York: The Macmillan Co., 1946.
A Grief Observed. New York: Bantam Books, 1976.
The Last Battle. New York: Macmillan, Collier Books, 1960.
Letters of C. S. Lewis. Edited with a memoir by W. H. Lewis. London: Geoffrey Bles, 1966.

Letters to Malcolm: Chiefly on Prayer. New York: Harcourt, Brace & World, 1964.

The Literary Impact of the Authorized Version. Philadelphia: Fortress Press, 1963.

Mere Christianity. New York: Macmillan paperback, 1960.

Miracles: A Preliminary Study. 1947. New York: Macmillan paperback, 1963.

Perelandra. 1944. New York, Macmillan paperback, 1965.

The Personal Heresy: A Controversy. With E. M. W. Tillyard. London: Oxford University Press, 1939. Oxford paperback edition, 1965.

The Pilgrim's Regress. 2d ed. Grand Rapids: Wm. B. Eerdmans, 1958.

Poems. New York: Harcourt, Brace & World, 1964.

The Problem of Pain. New York: The Macmillan Co., 1961.

Reflections on the Psalms. London: Collins, Fontana Books, 1958.

Selected Literary Essays. Edited by Walter Hooper. Cambridge and New York: Cambridge U. Press, 1969.

Surprised By Joy: The Shape of My Early Life. New York: Harcourt, Brace & World, 1956.

They Asked for a Paper. London: Geoffrey Bles, 1962.

Till We Have Faces. 1957. Reprint ed. Grand Rapids: Wm. B. Eerdmans, 1964.

Transposition and Other Addresses. London: Geoffrey Bles, 1949. (Also published as *The Weight of Glory and Other Essays.* New York: Macmillan paperback, 1965.)

The Voyage of the Dawn Treader. New York: Macmillan, Collier Books, 1970.

The World's Last Night and Other Essays. New York: Harcourt, Brace & World, 1960.

SECONDARY SOURCES

Black, Max, ed. *The Importance of Language.* Ithaca and London: Cornell University Press, 1962.

Carnell, Corbin S. *Bright Shadow of Reality.* Grand Rapids: Wm. B. Eerdmans, 1974.

Carpenter, Humphrey. *Tolkien: A Biography.* Boston: Houghton Mifflin Co., 1977.

Christopher, Joe R., and Ostling, Joan K. *C. S. Lewis: An Annotated Check List of Writings About Him and His Works.* Kent State University Press, 1974.

Cunningham, Richard B. *C. S. Lewis: Defender of the Faith.* Philadelphia: The Westminster Press, 1967.

Fuller Theological Seminary. *Theology, News and Notes.* Pasadena: Fuller Theological Seminary, 1976.

Gibb, Jocelyn, ed. *Light on C. S. Lewis.* New York: Harcourt Brace Jovanovich, 1965.

Gilbert, Douglas, and Kilby, Clyde S. *C. S. Lewis: Images of His World.* Grand Rapids: Wm. B. Eerdmans, 1973.

Henry, Carl F. H., ed. *Revelation and the Bible.* Grand Rapids: Baker Book House, 1959.

Holmer, Paul L. *C. S. Lewis: The Shape of His Faith and Thought.* New York: Harper & Row, 1976.

Hordern, William E. *A Layman's Guide to Protestant Theology.* Rev. ed. New York: Macmillan, 1968.

Kilby, Clyde S. *The Christian World of C. S. Lewis.* Grand Rapids: Wm. B. Eerdmans, 1964.

Kilby, Clyde S., ed. *A Mind Awake: An Anthology of C. S. Lewis.* New York: Harcourt, Brace & World, 1969.

Kreeft, Peter. *C. S. Lewis—A Critical Essay.* Grand Rapids: Wm. B. Eerdmans, 1969.

Lindsell, Harold. *The Battle for the Bible.* Grand Rapids: Zondervan Publishing House, 1976.

Lindskoog, Kathryn. *C. S. Lewis: Mere Christian.* Glendale: Gospel Light Publications, 1973.

————. *The Lion of Judah in Never-Never Land.* Grand Rapids: Wm. B. Eerdmans, 1973.

Montgomery, John Warwick, ed. *Myth, Allegory, and Gospel.* Minneapolis: Bethany Fellowship, Inc., 1974.

Moorman, Charles. *Arthurian Triptych: Mythic Materials in Charles Williams, C. S. Lewis, and T. S. Eliot.* Berkeley: University of California Press, 1960.

Reilly, R. J. *Romantic Religion: A Study of Owen Barfield, C. S. Lewis, Charles Williams, and J. R. R. Tolkien.* Athens: University of Florida Press, 1966.

Ryken, Leland. *The Literature of the Bible.* Grand Rapids: Zondervan Publishing House, 1974.

Schaeffer, Francis A. *No Final Conflict.* Downers Grove: Inter-Varsity Press, 1975.

Walsh, Chad. *C. S. Lewis: Apostle to the Skeptics.* New York: The Macmillan Co., 1949.

White, William Luther. *The Image of Man in C. S. Lewis.* Nashville: Abingdon Press, 1969.